WE MEET

KENNETH PATCHEN

BOOKS BY KENNETH PATCHEN
AVAILABLE FROM NEW DIRECTIONS

Collected Poems
In Quest of Candlelighters
The Journal of Albion Moonlight
Memoirs of a Shy Pornographer
Selected Poems
Sleepers Awake
The Walking-Away World
   Wonderings
   Hallelujah Anyway
   But Even So
We Meet
   Because It Is
   Poemscapes
   A Letter To God
   Hurrah For Anything
   Aflame and Afun of Walking Faces

KENNETH PATCHEN
We Meet

Preface by Devendra Banhart

 A NEW DIRECTIONS BOOK

Acknowledgement: Dear Michael Barron, my sweet editor, I could not have flung myself at this most
daunting of tasks if it weren't for your Olympian lexicon, boundless grammatical expertise, and
haunting turquoise trousers. Thank you.   —D.B.

Publisher's Note: *We Meet* collects five New Directions Kenneth Patchen titles: *Because It Is* (1946),
Poemscapes (1957), *A Letter to God* (1958), *Hurrah for Anything* (1960), and *Aflame and Afun of Walking
Faces* (1970), previously available only as separate editions.

Manufactured in the United States of America
Cover and front matter by Rodrigo Corral Design/Christopher Brand
Interior composition by Arlene Goldberg
New Directions Books are printed on acid-free paper.
First published as New Directions Paperbook 1115 in 2008

Library of Congress Cataloging-in-Publication data

Patchen, Kenneth, 1911–1972.
    We meet / Kenneth Patchen ; preface by Devendra Banhart.
       p. cm.—(New Directions paperbook ; 1115)
    ISBN 978-0-8112-1758-3 (pbk. : acid-free paper)
    I. Title.
    PS3531.A764A6 2008
    811'.54—dc22

New Directions Books are published for James Laughlin
by New Directions Publishing Corporation
80 Eighth Avenue, New York, NY 10011

CONTENTS

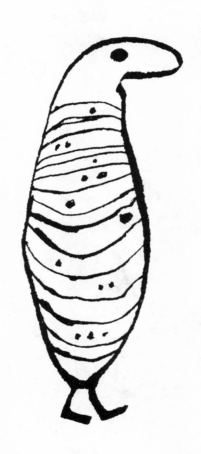

PREFACE

by Devendra Banhart

I came across Kenneth Patchen the way one dreams of a tumbleweed rollin' on by, leaving trails of luminosity from within its prismatic pit. The world is, of course, that damn tumbleweed with Patchen's riddle wrapped around itself, now here, now gone, like the marriage between "Hi!" and "So Long." We are left born before a new kind of page, the shit kicked out of us, and nothing is sweeter. . . . Blessed be this shitkicker.

This could happen to you. It happened to me and all I did was randomly pull from my little library Patchen's book, *Because It Is*. It's something I can only describe in a matter-of-fact sort of way because it was created in a matter-of-fact sort of way. This is poetry and art explored through the language of possibility, wisdom and humor. Within these pages, mystery becomes little cartoon legs with a cosmic giggle for a head, ramblin' out the difference between sincerity and honesty, reminding us that its one thing to have the gift but it's a whole other thing to GIVE it.

I'm nuts about Patchen, and I've never come across anything like his work. I live happily at the bottom of the totem pole of Patchen's devotees. Allen Ginsberg made a point to visit Patchen during his first trip to San Francisco. Henry Miller wrote an essay entitled "Man of Anger and Light" in his honor. Patchen worked with John Cage on an experimental radio play, "*The City Wears a Slouch Hat.*" Charles Mingus' quartet accompanied him during one of his few readings (a recording has never been found). Lawrence Ferlinghetti even wrote an elegy to Patchen after his death. The list grows on.

By now, if you were me, you'd be wondering who this guy was, so I'll tell ya' what teeny-tiny tidbits I know. Kenneth Patchen was born on December 13, 1911, in a little city in Trumbull County, Ohio, called Niles. In 1924, Niles was the setting for an 18-hour battle between The Ku Klux Klan and the anti-Klan organization, The Knights of the Flaming Circle. I don't know this for sure, but it's possible that the battle (which the Knights won!) had a great impact on his being an ardent pacifist. While still in college, Patchen's poem "Permanence" was published in *The New York Times*. It was his first published poem. What the fuck, right? After leap froggin' from college to college he met his true love Miriam Oikemus, to whom he would eventually dedicate every one of his 40 plus books. He was a rising star of poetry until an accident occurred while working on a friend's car that would debilitate him for life and eventually confine him to a wheelchair till his death in Palo Alto, California, on January 8, 1972.

Like confused clouds illuminating whatever the opposite of a shadow is, Patchen's painted-poems and written drawings highlight a rogue sensibility within our humanity. Every emotion, every joke, every creation jostles us. To experience his work is to discover a peculiar sort of divinity. Heed the wisdom of the first poem in this collection, *"to understand one must begin somewhere. . . . "* Welcome!

Poem for KP

The Silver Deer has appeared,
it's presenting itself,
its eyes are everyland,
its mouth milks a funny-kinda-heaven,
and knows the POEM can make the flame extinguish itself,
and knows the POEM is the circle surrounding all circles,
and it wants us to stop coddling the grumpy raisin,
to stop bobbing for beans in the house of "mama i can't leave this
body! but oh . . . !"
to stop pumping stones out of our lava-slits,
to welcome in the welcoming red thread, the lining,
the one who is reaching out to wherever the hell you are,
to not wait, to never wait again.

BECAUSE IT IS

for Miriam

BECAUSE *TO UNDERSTAND* *ONE MUST BEGIN SOMEWHERE*

John Edgar Dawdle married a little chicken
And went to live in a hatbox
Which stood near the castlewall; but
At five o'clock the king came and
Wanted to give them a thousand buttered Rolls-Royces,
Eighty barrels of turpentine-mellowed trout, a flute
Which he claimed had belonged to a W. R. Mozart,
And half a glass of rounded ale.
So, not wishing to appear rude or ungrateful,
They restrung his tennis racket, subscribed to
All his magazines, and each wrote PEACE
On his behind; for he'd hurried over
Without bothering to dress. Oh, he was fine!
And they all stayed there . . . except him,
And Dawdle, and the pretty little chicken.

BECASUE *THEY WERE VERY POOR THAT WINTER*

The only mother he could afford was a skinny old man
Who sat on the roof all day drinking champagne—
(The real stuff of course was much too expensive);
Previous to that, about a year later,
She joined the Society For The Placating
Of Polar Giraffes—and almost immediately discovered
That by earnestly pronouncing "Your coat's wet"
In Arabic, great numbers of drowned sailors
Would drop from the sky and dance
Through the streets until shot by cops.
So, being just turned three, little Coralou
Naturally bristled at her grandfather's suggestion that
They go together to the stationhouse and
Try the new lavatory facilities there. "Conscientious taxpayer,
Are you!" she snorted. "I suppose that's why you've
Got your overcoat pockets stuffed with snapshots
Of Martha Washington playing basketball on rollerskates!"
Obscure indeed are the vestments of destiny:
In the end, rose and ostrich smell much
Alike; and only the thinking of clouds
Keeps the world on its untroubled course.

BECAUSE *SHE FELT*
BASHFUL WITH PALM TREES

His father decided to rent a car
That had belonged to an old Gypsy;
And, in order to avert the risk,
Particularly in alleys and on enclosed bridges,
Of mustache-entanglement, to drive it backwards
Across the country. But when they opened
The trunk compartment, expecting to find there
A supply of used burro-stoppers—those
Staples of the Mexican stage—without which,
They had been cautioned, no Presidential audience
Could be in the completest sense satisfactory;
They were a little disappointed to find
Only a great blind white lion seated
On the very edge of the air.
There are days nobody gets a break.

BECAUSE *EVERYBODY LOOKED SO FRIENDLY I RAN*

Oh, the foxy chairabbit and the goofy beduck
They go out to buy a house of their own.
Oh, leave pretty little Melissa some, boys,
And let your golden rooster ride on Hallelujah's back
Till you perceive the weeping angel in that stone.
Oh, the spotless stovelephant and the grimy dishclothclown
They have gone to give their precious little damn about
The why and the wonder of the world; you do the same, boys!
Oh, lay it on the water, lean it on the wind;
We ain't got long, boys—it's about time we begin!
Oh, the kind of angel I'm on the side of
Won't ever try to hide from the terrible responsibilities of love!

BECAUSE *THE ZEBRA-PLANT*
BORE SPOTTED CUBS

He grabbed the beanpot off the clothesline
And poured hot maple syrup into his parade sneakers;
And still it was a mess! (Hear footnote above.)—
Like frantic horsemen trying to exchange nightgowns on a lake.
"Today," announced the kindlingwood, "September begins."
And the sinkstopper growled: "Wha-at! on April 10th!"
"It is a mite late this year," admitted a swansnail,
Ruffling up its shell and trying ineffectually to scowl.
"Shut up!" commanded Grover Clevewater Giraffe. "Let's
Everybody get on this here blade of grass;
Then the one with the handsomest neck will
Be given all the jellybuns. How's that?"
The old philosopher slowly lowered his stone:
"Suppose," he said, "you were a wisp of sour loneliness
Stuck to the wrong side of a life; would you right away
Have someone locked up for trying to lap your hand?
Someone, that is, who had spent thirty-five years
Pasting vile-tasting labels on cans in
A dog-meat factory. Yes, they say there are rooms;
That there are reasons; that things make sense . . . Yes, woof! woof!
But it will all come right; yes, it will end.
The last cruel wag to a cruel tale.
Ah, no . . . life is not a story that children
Should ever be allowed to hear about."

BECAUSE *ALL THE FORESTS WERE PLAYING LEAFROG*

I broke a corner off the house
And put an eagle egg on it; also
I took a pretty lilacat out. But
The Captain, the Captain's wrongsidein eyewhiskers,
Her shell-tan nightgown, and the Captain's
Lightbulbous nose, as well as the Captain's back sideyard,
Now caked with ticking birds and chambermaids
Grousing about yacht prices—all these, and
A minus-fifteen policemen; an agnostic mantis;
The first cousin of a backward but capital woC—
Little Wooly, their mixed-up and sheepish skoffring;
A dead steamshovel; Miss Mildred's dyeing gear, with
Special elixirs for those without hair, as well as baldies;
Together with a weaselark; a spoonful of extremely cool
Hot saucer solos; some rubbernails; and a full trapdoor
Guarded over by an unarmed honeysuckle bush—
All these were waiting for the train. What in hell are
You doing? What are you waiting for!

BECAUSE *I DIDN'T*
MEAN NO HARM, MISTER

They chased me off and it was
Getting lonesome and I couldn't recollect anything
Much except riding with an old battered Indian
Up to the fifth floor of an empty building
And being sort of surprised when he took a pheasant sandwich
Out of his very hip pocket and lent it to some fellows.
Another time I got locked in overnight in
A shoestore, I noticed a large big grasshopper
Came in pushing a shiny cartful of wheels;
But my mother was away visiting father,
And when neither of them got home for supper,
They just stretched out in a ditch.
"To melt thin syrup you need either
A smart fire or a pretty hairy wrist."—
That was the motto of our town 'paper,
But when I couldn't get work nobody ever caught
The editor giving up any of his liberal illmannerisms.
In this country it's still as easy for a worm
To turn into a bird as for a poor boy
To wish he had some wealth or money.

BECAUSE *THE STREET SAT THERE SCRATCHING HIMSELF*

I wanted to get a lion on the hat
So I placed the first wagon one full slice
From the end of the loaf; the boatshaft,
Counterpane, tapered drum, and the baggy climate,
I carefully wove into ridges, and the resulting stair
Into corners of fox and flax and gleaming satchel tacks.
Trees' hair . . . ribboning weave of birds . . . summer has
Some pretty fetching tricks up her sleeve. And up there—
Ah! you far out crazy daisies! It'll take some real circling
To square that field with any unified theory! UFO
And I'll PDQ (Provide the Dogstar Quills). In general,
Everything is unfathomably particular. Air has
Firmer bones than any beast, fish, or unheritable blossom.
Memory does leave strange lions on our hats . . .
When I worked in the Haggerstown quarry
The mules had red whiskers down to their knees;
Now the willows kneel glumly on the riverbank,
And no carts call, no cook's gong startles the squid.
Who remembers the timid house on Duggers Lane?
The only one for marvels around without
Roof, walls, doors, windows, tenants, or rooms.
Oh, who remembers Old Bob, the blind taxi driver?
Does anyone even remember what the near-sighted Eskimo said
When he came upon a shivering angel in a snowdrift?
Who today remembers Miss Mammy Tina? or Little Ragged Jeffie?

—And the showwindow of the taxidermist's just off Lubbert Alley,
Where, for seventeen motionless years, she held him on her lap?
No, alas . . . most of us have to keep pretty hopping and headsup
Just so as how our hats don't go slipping off under some cuspidacious bus.

BECAUSE *WE MAKE OUT WHEN WE'RE IN*

Most of his kinsfolk were related but
The druggist's sister would get hold
Of somebody she'd bend that person
The shape of a piece of lampwick
And tie him maybe ten feet or so
Off the ground right in the deepest
Part of the lake and you'd ask her
Why she did it, she'd always say
Tomorrow I'll take him to see
My lawyer if he likes; another boy
We knew at that time—a sort
Of nervous type named Ebbret,
Who, afraid of rabbits, went round
Disguised as a prickly carrot . . .
He was later eaten by a horse in Arizona—
Should also be mentioned here,
If only for the reason that his mother,
And his grandmother, and his great-grandmother,
Were all so ticklish that not only
Did they never marry, but it was worth
The arm of many an unsuspecting stranger
Just to venture a polite handshake with them
On the steps of the half-gutted townhall.

BECAUSE *THE FLYBYNIGHT* *PEERED INTO THE WASHTUB*

Poor Clerinda Soup sat on in Roanoke,
But they all quickly left again anyhow.
While drenched cyclists hung by their toes,
White panthers came from the wings bearing
In some cases feathers and in wooden jars
The prettily shingled songs of barnowls. Never
Were they happier than when I strolled
Into that hotel room only to find myself
And Clerinda floating past the open window;
Yet that half-quart keg containing fifty gallons
Of spiked Old Tigersnot had to be emptied twice
Before we could even get out of the world!
Oh, flaming pig in a frockcoat, blue mule with wings—
And we are but the shadows of still more shadowy things.

BECAUSE *SOMETIMES YOU CAN'T ALWAYS BE SO*

I never read of any enforceable regulation
Against removing orangeskins from apples in private;
But when my brother tried to buy
A sandwich in the Lodi post office yesterday,
One of the town's leading social blights
Bit him in the leg! Why, only last
Week an aunt of mine had a horse
Named Sesroh fall asleep on her shoulder
In the subway! The fifth Friday in July
A flagload of my cousins were arrested for pulling
A rowboat down the main drag in Yonkers—
Despite the fact it had cost them sixty bucks
To get the governor's grandmother drunk enough
To ride nude in it! Talk about patriotism!—
Is civic mindedness to be an empty catchsword
For every schoolboy to sneak his first shave with?
Are the hallowed drawers of our forefathers to be bulged
Thus shamelessly forth above every pawnshop in the land?
I believe it was Old Mother Frietchie who said:
"Shoot, son, even if I could dance,
There are a lot better ways to have a ball
Than scraping the hair off your own head."

BECAUSE *A DOOR*
IN THE HILL OPENED

An old man floated through the window
And landed in my soup. Before I
Could lift him out I noticed a
Small elephant seated on his head. But it
Wasn't until I had them comfortably settled
Before the fire that still another passenger
Revealed himself: a certain page-in-waiting
To the bookish Lady Tougai of Beddingham-on-Aiggs,
Who, while still a child, kept poor Roger Overnott
Waiting forty-nine years on the sunken balcony
Above the potting salon—an incident which
Led to the rather heated founding of Antzpantts
Near Blisterbotham (the township of pretty Dade County,
Where, as everyone knows, the repeating rifle
Was first introduced to a joyous populace
On Christmas Day, 1847.) "Tell me, sir," I said,
Hoping to ascertain whether I had to deal
With injury or simple affection, for the old man
Kept clapping his hand to the seat of his pants;
"Is anything amiss?" To which he answered:
"A miss? Hell no, it's my wife—she insists on
Keeping her damn snapping turtles in my back pocket!"

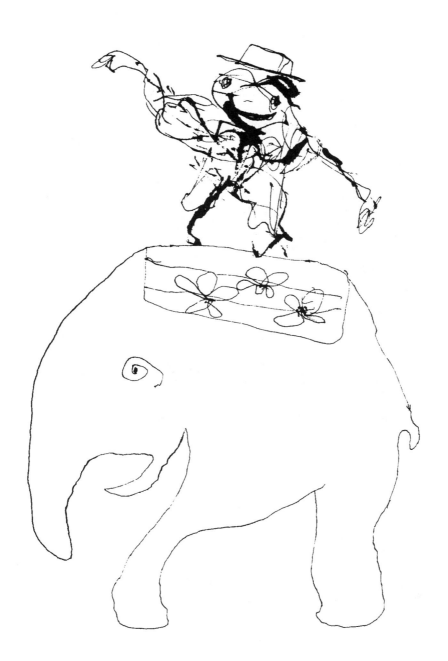

BECAUSE *A FIRTREE*
SHOOK HANDS WITH ORION

That famous Irish constellation, my birth-badge,
Only higher than my Scotch-kited grandfather at his
Melancholicly rollicking best; they felt it time
I learned from him about McKevin's curse,
And why the Countess had her belly
Painted that day beside the Cambrian Sea.
But first, since I was only six,
And of wayward temper, they took me
By a roundabout route to the meatbutcher's,
Where, between hands of Pilatatti, my cousins
Taught meditation, wig-powdering, and the several
Systems for preventing rain from falling upward;
As well as explaining—when they were
Of a mind to, which was never—
Why Mellifenza Galt Mertin refused to comment
When the milkman climbed into her bathtub.
But soon, purloined by a very curious tribe
Of Indians, we were escorted to Seattle, Maryland,
Then a missionary wickiup below Lake Friedrichskul—
And so I never saw grandfather, cousins, or myself again.

BECAUSE *GOING NOWHERE* *TAKES A LONG TIME*

Something in the climate of a hammer
Struck him when young. Call a
Sparrow a lamp, you'll still need
The liking of chairs to settle
What is at bottom only painted over
Cloth; and that flat cunning of plates,
How little it speaks above the soup's
So roundly directional bravura. Count the sky
A pan, you'll still be hard put to find
Any flash in its like. But ah, alas, alas,
Lottipo . . . the mushy marshes, those tree-lined woods,
The so-small journeying, and the trivial occupants thereof . . .
These, too, and all else, alas, are only real. So may we
Remember once again how the grasses cause the wind to move .
Ah, alas, dear Toppilo, what then is this realm that seems
So like a cell, without jailor or judge, or witness even . . .?
And that we love! is this not a proof of something!
No, I admit—not necessarily of heaven . . .

BECAUSE *THE GROUND-CREATURE* *LOOKED SO SAD*

The little green blackbird watched a sunflower
And a child's swing and an old woman crying.
So the tiger asked him if he'd seen
The little green blackbird around anywhere.
The tiger was there too, and also
A tiger just in from the forest.
Well, the little green blackbird also watched
A willow tree's birth and a winged crocodile too.
So then the lion asked him if he'd seen
The little green blackbird around anywhere.
You see, the lion was there too, and also
A huge bearded mouse that looked like a lion,
But was really a fat brown fish too lazy to shave;
In those days, only the most timid barbers took along
Their razors when they went in swimming.
But the little green blackbird felt pretty good
And he got himself a cuckoo named Willie Watt,
A baby whale named Willie Watt, and a big yeller hound dog
Which everyone called Willie Watt, but whose name
Was really Willie Watt; in those days, nobody minded.
So the flea's sister asked him if he'd seen
The little green blackbird around anywhere.

The flea's wife was there too, and also
An uncle of the flea's cousin's sister,
Who was also Willie Watt's father. You see, in those days,
Nobody minded and it was pretty nice.

BECAUSE *THE BOY-HEADED LARK PLAYED ONE*

The little green blackbird became quite anxious
To try the little-known guitar-trombone-ophone
For himself; however, before having a go at it,
He went up into the Great Smoky Mountains
And there meditated eleven years with nothing
To eat or drink except a variety of foods
And beverages. Then, one evening toward night,
It suddenly came to him to wonder
Why the sky was up above there; and also,
Whether, if he could stand on top of it,
The sky might not wonder the same thing about him.
So he ran lickity-split down the mountain
And told an old fellow on a bike about
His idea: (Of course at the time he didn't know
That the bulgy-legged old fellow was a train robber,
But when he got home his was gone . . . and only a few
Wisps of stale steam still clung round the cabin door.)
"Alas," said the little green blackbird sadly;
"I always thought it just another futility of speech,

That 'train of thought' thing. Oh well, I'll drop by
The Nightingale Café; perhaps Dolly and Kate and the Captain
Will be back from their wedding. Now, let me see . . .
'Accumulation' is a long word; and 'candles'
Is another, though its length is more variable."

BECAUSE *MY HANDS HEAR*
THE FLOWERS THINKING

I scooped up the moon's footprints but
The ground climbed past with a sky
And a dove and a bent vapor.
The other half of cling together wove by
In the breath of the willows; fall in
Sang eagle ox ferret and emerald arch.
O we, too, must learn to live here;
To use what we are. O fall in now!
For only love is community! Of various likenesses, none
Unless one love! In the lionleaf, the sonshade
Spreading over a father's road! When we love,
God thinks in us. And in that home-going time,
We see with the eyes of grass; and in the trees
Hear our own voices speak! So gently, gently, I say
That sleep is the secret-releasing key to this world.
Our lives are watching us—*but not from earth.*

BECAUSE *SUNSET CAME* *AT HALF-PAST NOON*

A spirited bookkeeper went to the courthouse
And, using a special paper, drew up
Warrants for the arrest and immediate apprehension
Of everyone in power . . . anywhere, anytime, for
Any and all reasons—including his own;
These noble, honorable, forthright, all-sacrificing individuals
Were then sealed in a leadcoated envelope
And rocketed up as a Christmas message.
Shortly after a bearded hand with several fingers
Bitten off at the knuckle drifted down.

BECAUSE *HIS SISTER SAW*
SHAKESPEARE IN THE MOON

The little green blackbird decided to study
Some history and geography; now, this meant going
To places like Portugal and Ayr Moor Gullibaad;
So he had some cards printed and
Handed them out. This of course started
A war, because the cards were printed
With ink. And the little green blackbird
Arrived in Portugal not only without cards,
But without a head, or arms, or legs,
Or even a little toe. This might not have been
So bad had he been feeling all right.
And it was no better in Ayr Moor Gullireet either;
In fact, it was just as sad really. "So much
For history and geography," he reflected
Ruefully; "but at least I'm a lot luckier
Than those poor unfortunates who still have heads
Left to think about what's going to happen to them."

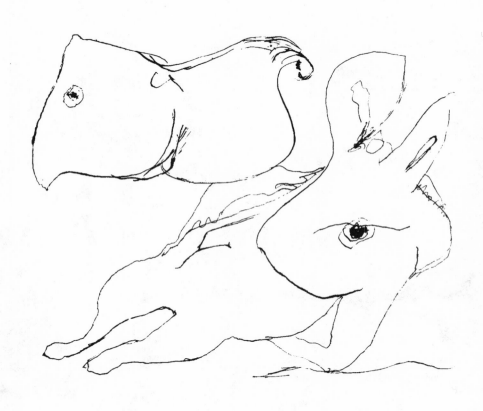

BECAUSE *HE KEPT IMAGINING A PENSIVE RABBIT*

The little green blackbird went off outdoors
And sat on a tree under a spreading chair.
When the sun came out it got dark
But the little green blackbird hadn't ever
Felt that lonely before and he laughed.
So some dinnerplates broke, the sun awoke,
The waitress in her flowered apron spoke;
And the little green blackbird sadly answered:
"If a friend of mine comes inquiring for me,
Tell him I've gone to join my grief
To the wintry crying of the northern sea."
And he leaned back with a puzzled smile,
Like the tiger amused by a sundial.
So the door closed, the rain closed,
The sun closed; also, the moon, a jar
Of raisin pudding, the tenth of January,
And half a raccoon. Now, alas, there was
Nothing left except the world; and nobody
In his right mind expects the world
To do anything now except close.

BECAUSE *HIS OTHER DOG*
WAS A HORSE

The kettlemaker's mother removed the bin but
Took away the bench; nevertheless, their son turned
Up under a field of swaying quiffpots
Who were trying to dry water on a cold fire.
The result was she married with her worst foot
Under the pillow, as the country people would say;
But do you think England, or Ecuador, or Sumatra,
Or even the so-called Friendly Islands where Mead,
Mook, and Tizzle wrote their memorable paper
On the significance of the coconut and the ripe banana
As referents in the erogenous conditioning of primitives;
Or even the judiciously considerate Solomon Group
Where Old Smiley Sigmund looked for a bloody boar
In the rushes and mistook his own reflection
For a dimpled little Moses, complete with long gray beard
And a frown to curdle the milk of a stone Madonna—
Do you think any of these even winced when they busted
Everything in her house that so much as hinted
That it had been made for any other reason
Than that it was cheap, and vicious, and of consummate hideousness?
If you do, I can't imagine how they'll ever be able to tell
When the moment comes to bury you.—But back to Genevieve:
She's found a really beautiful place to live;

And if you go there any time except Sunday or a weekday,
She'll be glad to show you—for the small price of your soul—
The very glove she caught the star you claim to be looking for in.

BECAUSE *HE WAS*
THINKING OF A BUMBLEBEE

The shoveltracker tossed the sand off again;
But the wormwood hare would not move.
Beside him lay the corpse of one
Named Zippity Jock, who had been hanged
For using chopsticks instead of buttonhooks
On a skittish customer in an East St. Louis
Corset fitter's shop; while above and below,
In the dried out shadow of the watertower,
Along the seams of Nellie Foophenjelly's sleepingbag,
On the tense knees and thumbs of fieldmice,
Inside the horns of odorously meditative cows,
Yes, and even under the frontporch swingamahickies
Of more than one roofed and glass-windowed house,
A small, goodnatured wind was beginning to blow.
Yet the shoveltracker went on with his work;
Interruptions meant nothing to him, or to his mother,
Whose hobby was giving imitations of a chicken swimming
On the tops of buses; nothing, nobody, could distract him!
At one point, a friendly bear with a disheveled, inky look
Sauntered up with the proposal that they mosey in to town
And tear up some lampposts together; another time,
A little man leading a kilted rhinoceros laden with shavingmugs
Offered him a part interest in The Pygmy Chamber Pot Company;

—Woops! he's struck water! And what's this he's lifting out?
Uh-ha! a half-drowned old hen with a pair of reading glasses
On her nose . . . and a mess of transfers stuck into her long gray feathers!

BECAUSE *HIS FRIEND CLAIMED* *THERE WEREN'T ANY*

The little green blackbird ran on and on
Until he chanced to meet a little green blackbird.
But the little green blackbird couldn't get
His car to work and so he said,
"Will you come to my house at seven?
Mike and Ellie are there right now;
However, if they don't show up, Joe Bill
Has promised to rub fresh mud into
Our shirts over behind the new schoolhouse."
"And what will that cost us?" asked
The little green blackbird, adjusting his thumbs.
"Only fifty apiece," answered the little green blackbird.
"Besides, I'm not so sure I like your attitude!
Obviously you're drunk. Here, help me up."
So the little green blackbird drove off
Down the road until he reached a bridge;
Then, adjusting his cap, and his thumbs,
He said, "What are you doing in that river?"
And the little green blackbird replied sharply,
"Waiting for Joe Bill's sister, that's what!
She comes here every Tuesday to wash his shirt."
"But this is Tuesday," the little green blackbird
Snorted, pausing to adjust his parade hat,
His honey-bee-striped hip-length socks,

His bright red paper wading boots, and
His well-worn thumbs; "You must be drunker
Than I thought!" And he drove into the lake.

BECAUSE *IT'S GOOD*
TO KEEP THINGS STRAIGHT

Now the little green blackbird liked a mouse
And a Malayan sunbear and a horse
And a beetle and a mouse and a horse
And a mouse and a leopard and a beaver
And a black fox and a fox squirrel and a lion
And a buffalo and a beaver and a donkey
And a tiger and a gorilla and a panther
And a salamander and a periwinkle and an ox
And an elephant and an alligator and an armadillo
And a mouse and a mule and a beetle
And a moonfish and a buffalo and a snail
And a horse and a lion and a butterfly
And a horse and a tiger and a mouse;
And the leopard and the donkey and the horse
And the buffalo and the ox and the elephant
And the mouse and the beetle and the gorilla
And the horse and the periwinkle and the mouse
And the panther and the lion and the tiger
And the butterfly and the beaver and the snail
Also liked the little green blackbird;
But the horse and the armadillo and the lion
And the buffalo were quite indifferent to him;
While the beetle and the mouse and the moonfish

And the salamander and the mule and the beaver
Didn't care one way or the other about him;
Whereas the mouse and the horse and the mouse
And the tiger didn't even know he existed.

BECAUSE *GROWING A MUSTACHE* *WAS PRETTY TIRING*

The little green blackbird's father always said:
"A bear and a bean and a bee in bed,
Only on Bogoslof Island can one still get
That good old-fashioned white brown bread!" This made a
Very deep impression on the little green blackbird,
So he decided to forget the whole thing.
But first he painted a stolen motorcycle on the sidewalk
And sold it to a nearsighted policeman.
By then of course the little green blackbird
Remembered that his father also did impressions
Of J. Greenstripe Whittier on freshly-painted parkbenches.
So he invited nineteen hundred rabbits over for dinner;
And they each brought him a tin-plated goldfish,
A handful of gloves, the drawing of a frosty breath,
And one of those decks of newfangled playing cards,
The kind that bite people. Well, when it came time
To go home, all nineteen thousand rabbits filed out
In a pregnant silence, that was broken only
By the sound of their low-pitched voices
Raised in speech. Whereupon the father
Of the little green blackbird quietly said:
"It is our sentence, to endure;
And our only crime, that we are here to serve it."

BECAUSE *ABOVE THE CLOUDS*
LITTLE FROGOOSES FLOATED

The Countess Cherrywhite left her shoeshine stand
And hurried down to Texas; within three
Minutes the mad dentist was back: "Come,"
Said he, brandishing his drills, "it's time
For your haircut, dearie." (Actually her head
Was still bandaged from the last one;
Even her dog, her parrot, her goldfish,
Her fryingpan, and her vacuum cleaner were
Still heavily swathed in gauze; her brother
In Weehawken kept his toupee in a vault—
And his neighbors on either side carried
Sawed-off shotguns even to the dinnertable.)
"Look-it here, you!" the Countess Cherrywhite protested;
"Dey got laws dat say no boy
What's not in his right mind can
Molest innocent folks lessen he's provided wit'
De proper Christian license to snuff dem out
On a rational, scientific basis . . . at a million or two
A clip, by Gar!"—Back at the
Shoeshine stand, Thanxamilion Boruschloski,
A self-employed idler, and perennial viewer with a-charm,
Stole a cheap look at the stars,
Said in a conspiratorial whisper to a passing statesman,
"I think we'll make it all right,

If mothers like yours go out of business soon enough."
—And smiled broadly. (Which was no mean feat,
Since he was only three and a half tall.)

BECAUSE *THEIR BELLS*
NEVER TOLLED THE TRUTH

Oh, the duchess combs her mirrored boredom
From the whore's son elegance of her lair;
But if I had my proper choice, boys,
I'd put most of here over there.
Oh, the rich man's got his troubles,
And the poor man's got some too;
But if I had my say about it, kiddies,
I'd kindly tell them both a few.
For the world is just as lousy rotten
As people damn well want it to be.

BECAUSE *WHERE THEY PLANTED SKYGREEN LEOPARDS GREW*

She raced along the timbers of a
Rosebud and there was a cardgame going
On and also a sorrow-rue between two
Old landladies contemplating the handiwork of
Their most out-of-head tenants—
But the party in the orchard
Was something else!—all those he-goats
Had clumb up to the bottom of
The well expecting to have their hats
Tuned, and maybe sneak a look at
The Bobbsey Twins getting booted out of
Some sportinghouse for insisting on single fares;
However, when a lumberjack with checkered spats
And waffle-proof knickers invited them to
Tea on page 287 of Catullus' *Private Capers*
Of Randolph Makepuce Emerywheel—while the piano
Temptingly played ragtime on their tossing ribs—
They were not at all surprised to hear that
Two handmaidens had just been pinched for being gloveless.

BECAUSE *THE NERVOUS VINE* *WOULDN'T TWINE*

He and they and the ladderleaner's step-niece
Charged into the forest to rub elbows;
It was still pretty soapy but not all geese
Drink wine in the summertime. "Well, Jason,"
The first soldier said, "expect a lot more
Of my kind along; we'll add a bit of real color—
Show man the pretty water that's in him; get to the core
Of his nasty little apple; brighten his pallid wool;
Give him the peace that only comes with war."
So, since that sounded completely disgusting,
They got right at it: hack, hack, hooray!
And up on Mars they damn near
Died laughing. I suppose from that distance
Caesar's backside does look about as fetching,
And kissable, as an elbow in the ground;
Whereas here, of course, it's the holiest artifact of our civilization.

BECAUSE *SOMETIMES THE HANDWRITING EATS AWAY THE WALL*

Oh the trash disposal unit shlupps happily
Through a stack of Mozart—as arranged for
Hi-futility Disneyphone; and the yawning deep freeze
Settles ever further into the Bloodywood bed.
A one-ah, two-ah—
O poor Charlie and Jane,
They went off on that midnight train;
While lucky Sue and Mr. Brown,
They stayed right there in the burning town.
For the star-spangled bull has swallowed the tiddlewink,
And the chrome-plated devil stirs in the kitchen sink.
So God bless the riders and the residers,
And the in- and the outsiders too;
'Cause it'll all be a lot like it is right now,
If that's left up to the likes of me and you.
For the worst and the best work together now as a team . . .
As the mushroom-hungry devil strides through that valley so green.
Yeah! the Loonies! the Loonies are really loose!
And it's much, much later and lousier than anybody thinks!

BECAUSE *THE SMALL MAN*
WAS A STRANGER

The friendly **greet**ing **ch**icken said, "Will you
Join me in a dish of *sleepy* grapes?"
"If you're quite sure there'll be room
For both of us," the *s*mall *m*an replied.
"It's been so long since I've eaten,
Something seems to fly out each time I open
My *mouth*." On the dark meat of the sky
Bright dabs of mu*s*tard began to appear,
And a *moo*dy fol*lowing* of *crows* accompanied
Them to her door. Once safely inside
The *s*mall *m*an banged his head
On a *beam* and proceeded to fall
Into a sewing basket on the *couch*.
"Hush," the **greet**ing **ch**icken said. "Oscar's asleep."
And she pointed to a tiny b*owl*
On the table. The stranger thought it
Damn odd to call a bowl Oscar.
But wanting to be polite, he said,
"Excuse me, did you say something about
Eating some grapes?" She looked at him in wonderment:
"What! after I've just got their little tails all curled,
And their pretty red bottoms tucked in for the night!
Come, Oscar—you can't trust anybody these days."
And sadly she sped away with her blinking b*owl*.

BECAUSE *MR. FLOWERS THE BOATMAN SAILED WALLS*

The Kumbria-Doggo began to sing again:
"Oh, they got up and sat so quietly,
All the dead who do not speak;
Though oak leaves grow on the oak,
And now and then a mouse does squeak."
Sam asked a riddle which none could doubt:
"If psalter and scepter season Caesar's broth,
What's the weight of a dead bird's thought?"
To which Bess, his nicest of kin, replied:
"As well a sea without looking as
Maid without your doing! O merry me,
And I shall smack plum in mysteries be!"
But the Boatman paid no mind, not he;
For wisdom is its own price in such peaceful company.

BECACUSE *THE WHOLE WORLD* *WAS ON FIRE*

A little owlion named Tom Birkis Jonnes
And a shy gorillapple named Miss Hazel Hurryweather
Raced like mad all the way to the moviehouse
But it was some corny picture about these
Crooks riding on a train and an
Old woman keeps getting drunk so the
Ski troopers search everybody and just
At the border who should appear but
Twelve guys with hair on the outside
Of their hats and they don't even
Have a chance to start dealing when
A big dog in a jellyglass face suddenly
Comes on deck and machineguns the audience;
So Tom Birkis Jonnes and Miss Hazel Hurryweather
Were certainly glad they'd gone to the woods instead—
For there they met many nice friends and
Had much good talk and after a while
Got married and ate supper and some delicious pies.

BECAUSE *TODAY'S MONKEY* *MAY WELL BE TOMORROW'S TUESLOCK*

I carted the steeple-knocker over there,
And I nailed another egg about here.
There seemed to be a horse waving
About four feet above Chicago, but damn
Little doing around Linwood. For one thing,
The disinterest rates were so out of line that
Of all my nine brothers only one
Was born with shoes on; and he
Had to fill out several tricky questionnaires
Before his first powder was even dry.
Small wonder my Uncle "Auntie Boo" Bludwater
Always said if they'd let everybody ride
Free on Lincoln's birthday you'd soon put
A stop to razorblade advertising on passenger trains.

BECAUSE *THERE ARE*
ROSES, SWANS AND HERBUGAZELLES

The lanterneater's daughter went to a banquet
Dressed as the phone number of an elm tree;
And they placed some angry bottles in array,
Set twelve runners to making boot soup—
Now don't shove me! interrupted Sam Bluesnow—as
The sideboard stifled a yawn; but the booths
Of the cuttlefishthieves and the short-wheeled carts
Of the pigmypigvendors took off like burning shirts.
(A word about screens: flies. Even in Skymirrortown
People got legs like U, only they're upside down.)
Oh, the lanterneater's daughter she sits all alone;
Not much she can do to stop what's been done.
For the leaves they fall on the moving water,
And the wedding guests are all dead and gone.
Oh, winter's chill dust will blight every green—
And Sam may cry but Sam will die.

BECAUSE *IN THIS*
SORROWING STATUE OF FLESH

They were hopeful of a curtain raiser
That would not sputter off in walls
And worklands instinct with shadows before gates
Where all helmets and orders eventually collect;
But none went to himself fully or
Made his might little enough to bear
The green loaves in his hand of leaves.
"All memory is piecemeal murder;
The hater in the mirror, it has a mother's impersonal gaze . . ."
"I do not think of the shorelights blurring out,
Or of the gray and raging glee
That slates these waves; but only
Of her tiny delicacy, of the strange gentleness of her fingers . . .
And of how very odd it is
That my man's heart should now be torn right out of me!"
"But the event itself, it has no speech; nor has it
Any meaning or purpose outside its own being. For existence
Is an animal substance, indivisible, and hence, unknowable;
And all things—stars, brides, and apple boughs—
And non-things, too—such as "history's happenings"—
Are but its cells and bones and tissues."
"And the voice of the father, there is no mercy in it;
All that vast chemistry of the sun . . . and little birds freeze!"
"I do not now think so much of what may only be idly argued;
For it seems a fact still of some importance, that I am dying."

BECAUSE *IT DIDN'T*
LIKE THE STORY ANYWAY

I stuffed the letter behind the pumphandle
And instructed the judge: you must choose
Between flashing about in trolleycars, both to
Left and just arrived, and making a
Silly basketlunch of yourself everytime some
Otter decides he bonny well won't. The neck
Of a floor loomed above the enwraptured lovers;
A cluster of peels appeared, seeking their
Friendly, nomad fruit; and Doctor Miransoli, dapper
As a noose, clumped lackadaisically into a field
But didn't pick any. Old Boy Blue
Up there, he don't seem to blow much
'Cept trouble; now, I ain't never been dead,
The little livin' man said; but I sure
Been double-deep in dyin' since I's born . . .
If there's anybody up there plays my tune,
They better get round to it pretty soon,
'Cause this jive 'bout some tree-foot unicorn
Don't music up no gravy on my spoon . . .
Man, them words just don't fit where I'm walkin';
How can I dig some corny waltz from some way-in horn
When all the deaths of my life are wailing at once?
And the judge said: "You know, there's something pretty fishy
About all you half-spitted Jonahs."

BECAUSE *TO REALLY PONDER*
ONE NEEDS WONDER

The moralistic Mrs. Winklemudjer called me to say
That in 1800 something an Abia Luw who
Lived on a private pension had a sort
Of table-like affair in his house
Where on a summer evening two ladies
Of the town indulged with him in dinner
And later being joined by an officer
Of the police his wife his mother together
With her youthful aunt's lover attired in folds
Of some stretchable cloth and armed with flowered bands
They all proceeded to an attic-cellar that was situated above
And slightly apart from the dwelling's other rooms
Staying there until their presence somewhat waning
They again went below bearing through physiological
Corporeality a marked resemblance to those kinds
Of group-individuals met with on cathedral balconies
At bird-watcher-watcher furtivities amongst deacon-duckers
Gallowsed-grandpa-goosers and before behind and between
Those railings of wood and temperament and plasticized steel
As we have come through mutual and understanding disparagement
To know them all too ill; at which point
A thatched roof two or three loafers from the bakery
Developed a low snore somewhere under its peak—

Now, as I think Homer or T. Cosfelder said:
You know, lads, the trouble with even the best story is,
It all too seldom tells what happened to us.

BECAUSE *A COW*
CHEWED OFF THE TRAINWHEELS

They abandoned their search for white coal
And walked across the Pacific on their
Hands and knees, thus avoiding unwary submarines;
However, just off Haverstraw, in a tremendous
Cave filled with chimneypots, matchsticks, and bagpipes,
They came upon a hippopotamus eating Edam cheese
And disclaiming: "I am your daughter Ricky Rudolph,
Arrived here yesterday by this morning's plane.
Go run and warn the rain, good pals; oh kindly do:
I don't want his little coat to get all wet too!"
And lo! the eyeless wind itself then said:
"There are crumbs for the birds; for the lion
In his golden sleep, such Africas
As make the very sky to weep;
For all some tiny, secret each . . .
And they be laid beyond reach . . .
Owls, oxen, elm, yew, and keening beech . . .
But for me, alas, there's only what all men dream of . . .
Myself the realm of restlessness; the dark love
Of the waters; the sun's mask whirling through
The emptiness; the blind, doughy face grinning
Above the thinking void—where unimaginable wonder
Stirs with every breath of every living thing!
And life and God—and branch and star—and they be gone . . .
And they be gone and dead, as for all of you they will . . .

And I alone am left . . . I, the wind . . . and that shall be enough . . .
Oh, that shall be enough to start the wonder of the dark,
The bright deep of that pale visitor
Whose hair I move . . . I, the wind . . . the bird's messenger
From that other world where no being need ever mourn."
And lo! from the heavens stepped a Sorrowing Child,
And said: "Long ago a butterfly was murdered,
And the wound of it resounds through the flesh of the universe
Forever; nerve ends of grass and trees and stars
Have sped that tiny death beyond the compass
Of any man's heart to touch it back into place.
—Not that murder is done, but that it is!
For death itself is murder; however birds sing."
And the improbably wonderful hippopotamus
Went on smiling into its plate of cheese.

BECAUSE *EVERYBODY'S CLOCK*
KEEPS A DIFFERENT TIME

Harney Harcole zipped downstairs just in time to
Grab hold of himself leaving by the roof;
But even then Maverna Vealle bowed her head,
Saying: "No! I shall not put it aside—
My cloak, cowl, and leg-blade, all in one!
Stop sniveling, mother! the joint is closed—
Locked, docked, jicky-pocked; besides, you've
Got enough load on right now to sink
The Maine and most of New Hampshire."
O night that nibbles . . . And darkness feeds
On the dark. The huddled figures.—Booom!
That time it was only a clock. The next, it may be the count-down.
Ten nine eight seven . . . Men birds and little fishes in the sea . . .
O where are the horsemen of light!—Booom!
The barroom, dark; the kingsroom, dark; the park, dark;
O the world and the water . . . *six five* . . .
Now have love and reason lost!—*four three* . . .
O the candlelight and the larks!—Booom!
And the ten doomed little Indians . . .
And the ten poor, doomed little Indians
Who have now become everyone on earth.

BECAUSE HE LIKED
TO BE AT HOME

He usually managed to be there when
He arrived. A horse, his name was
Hunry Fencewaver Walkins—he'd sometimes
Be almost too tired to make it;
Because, since he also hated being alone,
He was always on the alert to pop forth
At a full run whenever the door opened.
Then one day it happened—
He didn't get there in time!
Of course he couldn't risk opening the door—
So, panting, he just stood there in the hall—
And listened to the terrible sound of himself weeping
In that room he could never, never enter again.

POEMSCAPES

P O E M I S C A P E

1) FASHIONED IN LOVE

Let it be fashioned in love! Boundless and imperturbable. Let it be! O tiger sleeping in the rose-heart. Let it be! Masterless, remote, solitary. A country where men and birds may come to take breath.

THAT COMES HERE! (2

I live in wonder. It is a glory to be alive in me. How there is grief! How there is grief and joy! O how there is a grief and a joy in me! The cursing prayer that is me! O far on the other side of me, beyond senses' reach — *that* comes here!

3) LIFE IS PRAISE

O unto me be given praising's gift! Wonder and love! O wonder and love!

AND GIVE BREATH (4

Beautiful are the trees, and the fields, and the waters. . . beautiful are the arms and throat of a woman. . . beautiful is the light on this table here. . . beautiful there in the sky. . . *Life is only beautiful.*

POEM **II** SCAPE

5) THE DANCING CHANCES

Throughout there is flowing. Statues, groves and stars. Nothing is still. All things are a returning. If we are to be all right, we must be getting ready to take something good back with us. Now.

CERTAINLY ENOUGH CUPS (6

The room is gay with cups. Thousands and thousands of them, big ones, little ones, clay, tin, china — there are even fifty of stone. The man who lives here is a cup, his wife is a cup. Their children are all cups except the oldest who is a saucer, and even he's cup-shaped.

7) ONE GRAY MORNING

"Dear friends" you are, at times, quite far away — after a manner of speaking.

FOG ROLLING IN (8

Old and forgotten they lie, ladies of all yesterday's evenings. Their noses and shanks bandaged with dirt; so. And with kings and sparrows. Today is June 18th. Nothing is ever stilled; in sorrow, in joy. . . *Flowing.*

POEM III SCAPE

9) THE LITTLE ESSAYS

Why Have Hands? They are, from time to time, useful. This has been, in many cases, established. They are mankind's only really trustworthy vocabulary, the nerves and muscles of the spirit made manifest. — Basically gay, unscientific.

MORE FABULOUS ANIMALS (10

This little fellow will delight you with his enthusiasm! He considers it a mark of special esteem to run up one's leg in search of spices which are an indispensable item of his fare. These he will find after arduous and oftentimes dangerous expeditions. One of a kind, his mating habits remain largely illusive.

11) GOLDEN PLUM BUDS

She loosens her hair. Out in the garden the flowers try on new colors.

MY JOURNEY'S JOURNEYING (12

Stand off! shouted the guard. Broken arrows bending up out of the silver quiver. . . He fired again and again across the harbor at us, the bullets glinting through the spongy tips like eyes in a bucket.

13) HOUSE OF TRIFLES

Pleasing and menacing, a house of trifles, and yet it must be possible to install a fountain somewhere. Sort of thing has been done, in the past at any rate. A fountain of rich, jetting blood.

THE LITTLE ESSAYS (14

Beethoven vs Statistics. Of course it requires little ingenuity to smell up quite a case against numbers. The case for them is likewise strong, however. What is the puzzled spectator to do? We know that Beethoven walked through parks with his hands in his pockets. This is the *practical* side to things: all else — minus a *plus*-ME.

15) THE BLIND WASHERWOMAN

Every evening she puts her pay into a flowered neckerchief and shuffles dustily drinkward.

GOLDEN PLUM BUDS (16

And now it is your grace that I would celebrate, O my flowering one. . . The roses walk upon the summer breeze never more lightly than thou upon these drab lanes of the village. . . Village? Nay! Paradise!

POEM **V** SCAPE

17) MORE FABULOUS ANIMALS

Nesting in threes, they waggle their long, skinny, yellow legs crazily about them. The females are usually very lazy, so nothing will do but somebody else lay their eggs. But in the nest, oh what jolly fun!

MY JOURNEY'S JOURNEYING (18

I am descended from a traveling people. Nothing would do but they go! They would travel any time of year, *anywhere*. "Let's go . . . Get going!" A kind of fermentation, a rash to the feet. But all I like about travel is getting out of places; the better the place the better I like scramming.

19) MY JOURNEY'S JOURNEYING

The yellow sponge of a streetlight in the rain. . . Gangrenous wounds of their cities. . .

MY INNOCENT COMPANIONS (20

This particular pair are constantly disappearing. One minute they're leaning out the window, laughing, calling something down to the postman; the next they've disappeared, leaving absolutely no trace. Once disappeared, they invariably, instantly, disappear again.

POEM VI SCAPE

21) THE TEMPLED LAMPS

The rain is falling. On the land, a disconcerting glitter of unimportantnesses — wagons, dogs, men. If it were not for the wide, chambered waters — so prudent, so renewingly clean — World, world, the lamps blurring out, out. . .

AN EXTRAORDINARY COMPLAINT (22

It is ruined, that admirable trade. Even the potato-appraiser can hold up his head on certain occasions, or hire somebody to do it for him. Not so with us. We are not shunned exactly, we are even much sought after in some circles; in fact, rather too much is made of us i s c.

23) THE VAST SHELTER

O the tiny red roofs there! the beautiful dynasty of flesh. . . Sing on, Heart!

ANOTHER DAY GONE (24

The sky is full of rain, a straining sack. A wet smell fills the house. I see that the light is thickening: on faces, an inch and a half; on things — carriages, trees — a good three-four inches.

POEM VII SCAPE

25) THE LITTLE ESSAYS

Meaning of Objects. Liberty is not often thought of as an object, like a bruised apple for instance. But liberty is all-important; liberty is more all-important than anything. Hence liberty is the only *object*-object.

THE LITTLE ESSAYS (26

What is "Names"? Whenever this problem arises, it is necessary to maintain a nice perspective. For it is desirable to examine the thing carefully, possibly (even) get furiously involved in it. This business of "names" is killing the world, you know. Not all at one stroke, but miserably, snivelingly. Behind the masks, rot, corruption, hypocrisy.

27) MORE FABULOUS ANIMALS

When sunlight hits a green leaf just right, that makes him! Abundant in children.

MY INNOCENT COMPANIONS (28

Rarely discerned in marshy ground, they wear customarily great, elongated shoes which set them apart in any company. As though to compensate for this eccentricity of dress, they wear nothing else whatever. Magnificent sliders; leather-connoisseurs.

POEM VIII SCAPE

29) LOVE IS PLAYFUL

Love is playful, noble and ennobled, O shattering gentleness! the sober, sweet glee of its flowing wonder! O love is playful and undesigning! Ah, wrath of it, the wrath of a man's love seeking its channel!

THE WOODS MAIDEN (30

Early one evening I met the maiden of the wood. Leaves and stars like cold leaves were twined in her hair. Sorrow stood on her face as a music, and through her walking sounded the weeping of birds. Behind her, his horns raking the sky, strode a great black stag. In silence they passed.

31) SOMEWHERE IS FLEETING

"My" life — Out of the silence the first flakes of snow begin to fall. . .

THE HEART'S LANDSCAPE (32

In loving tenderness, whisper of flesh through the darkening curtain. . . Sorrow's music taking flight through these soft folds. . . In loving tenderness (and secret anguish), O intricate intentions, banners waving above invisible fortresses. . . Horizon of retreating silhouettes. . .

POEM IX SCAPE

33) YOUNG GIRLS SWIMMING

Bodies like wavering, half-dissolving flowers, young girls swimming in the river. There! the pink, silken petal of a thigh! the clustering loveliness of a tiny breast! How very blue and pure the sky above them.

SOMETIMES IS NEVER (34

At the moment when the player for the highest stakes walks naked in the garden and there is no certainty for him and the tombs of youth echo only the decaying tramp of causes lost before attempted and the tigers on the shadowy riverbank cry piteously in their sleep and the chips prove counterfeit.

35) IN SUCH HARNESS

Out of the river rides a naked girl, shoulders of her horse star-lathered. . .

ONE SUMMER NIGHT (36

I formed a shawl of the water's shining, a clasp from a seabird's wing. . . for the skirt I took the mist from over a summer field. . . and with these I clothed her. . . her heart beating, *beating*. . .

P O E M **X** S C A P E

37) GOLDEN PLUM BUDS

This night the wind moves almost without sound through the leaves of the tree beneath my window. I think of many things I would not willingly remember. The wind moves very quietly. The leaves hardly stir.

THE LITTLE ESSAYS (38

Wherefore & Henceforth. There is no disputing the miserable showing of the "average intelligence." Too often the inclination is rife to formulate principles along whose narrow highways some congress in "harmonious evaluations" may be precipitated, or at least partially *behaviorized.* This is palpable poppycock! Where does this leave INSTINCTIVE INSTINCT? Time somebody thought of that!

39) AT THIS MOMENT

As I say this a flashing wheel of children spins across the sun-drenched lawn!

A NIGHT SONG (40

When did my letter reach you? Had you already found the room you longed so hard for, or were (are) you still looking? I told you something in the letter I didn't mean to. — No matter.

POEM XI SCAPE

41) AID TO DELIVERANCES

As an aid to deliverances, though by nature grave and troubled, the Guardian of the Wall, whose own deepest, purest wish. . . alas, alas, alas. . . by a terrible excess of gaiety *he will love and help you*.

KINDNESS OF CLOWNS (42

The clowns have built a house in the forest, by sheer jest of numbers. Then they want to move a clown from an alien league into it. Until that moment no one had ever shown that clown any kindness, so naturally he was suspicious. His father said those fellows plan to steal your pants.

43) KINDNESS OF CLOWNS

(The father cannot be blamed for his suspicions. Bad blood existed between the leagues.)

KINDNESS OF CLOWNS (44

But father's and son's suspicions were unfounded. The forest-living clowns moved their rival into the house and fed him delicious foods and let him win all the card games. This treatment made him more suspicious.

POEM XII SCAPE

45) NOT CHERISHED ENOUGH

I do not feel that it is cherished enough, this hesitant thing, shy under the fingers' touch. Planted in almost any soil, it would thrive, grow raptly sunward. More courageous than a lioness; more beautiful, too.

MY INNOCENT COMPANIONS (46

They are tirelessly searching for large bodies of dry water. In apartment houses, grain storagetanks, garages in the suburbs, literally anywhere, look closely and you are bound to spy them, their arms waving like antennas, noses stretched with sniffing, keen on the scent, positively enraptured! And what's more, they always *do* find them!

47) GETTING UP EARLY

Such a marvelous delicacy of castles shimmering out upon these bushes in the morninglight. . .

WHEN THAT HAPPENS (48

At no other call! Cherished at its *real* level! How joyous! How truly joyous! Even the touch of the fingers turning into curious plants that drink thirstily of the sun! Every nerve strumming like a wing!

POEM XIII SCAPE

49) THE FLUID APPEARANCES

Faithful to what enchants me. . . The rosy, singing fire of the living flesh! how splendid! O how splendid! what dazzling consolations! temptations! such durable halos! Today I'm lost in a mingling of fluid appearances. . . imperishable audacities. . . !

GOLDEN PLUM BUDS (50

Since it is as beautiful as it is, there will be nothing done in vain in this world. When it lay across my hand, the ardent glow of noon upon it, reverently, barely touching it, as a golden mouth lightly touches a forehead fashioned of cobwebs, I seemed to have entered an unsuspected portal.

51) SURROUNDED WITH ENCHANTMENTS

In the caress of shapes, colors, immaculate appearances. . . O we are surrounded with enchantments!

ABOUT MAKING JUDGMENTS (52

Well, I have not reserved judgment, that would be a terrible nuisance, my spirit could never stand it. I have, instead, made judgments about an astonishing number of matters. At their head: Who can judge anything?

53) THE PICKLED CHAFFINCH

Destiny unmakes strange bedfellows. There was once a great number of people hastening to an inn. "Plenty rooms" they kept saying. Actually there were only three. Moreover, the inn was closed for seasonal repairs and refurbishments.

THE LITTLE ESSAYS (54

Is Destiny Desirable? Fortunately an answer to this question will depend entirely on each individual's own presentiment. Some will endeavor to sidestep; others to deck themselves out in vague discretions, alluding perhaps to example, foreign to any normal experience. Nobody can really blame either faction: destiny, let's face it, is either desirable — or it is *undesirable*.

55) WHAT DESTINY DESIRES

Destiny is the music of the improbable. Were it otherwise, almost anyone could exist.

KINDNESS OF CLOWNS (56

Destiny made a shambles of their playful house in the forest. In the guise of a cyclone, followed by a violent explosion. The clowns and their reluctant guest (him of the rival league) scattered without further ado.

POEM XV SCAPE

57) MY INNOCENT COMPANIONS

Perpetually leaping up and refusing to recognize chairmen. (As you know we have meetings here right along, every few minutes practically. Sometimes within a meeting there'll be a dozen other meetings. — "Who's that bum!" — "*Sit down!*"

MY JOURNEY'S JOURNEYING (58

Suppered at the inn. Nervous with those thousands of massive candles which walk lumberingly about between the tables, squirting a foul-smelling stuff out of their ears and guffawing uproarously each time the innkeeper drops a plate or a diner, braver than his fellows, openly expresses resentment at one of their unusually crass overtures.

59) WHAT STARTS WELL

They began by discussing the charming shoulders of bottles; ended seated on their own.

FRIEND THE RABBIT (60

Once outside the door we chanced to meet a rabbit on muleback going from house to house trying to sell shares in an unbigening block of ice. Mopping our brows, we wished him all the best.

POEM XVI SCAPE

61) KINDNESS OF CLOWNS

No sooner had the clowns got a new house built, a worse wind than the first blew it down. And it also re-blew down the old house which they had scarcely begun to prop up.

FRIEND THE RABBIT (62

The special, brilliant, ebullient way he rode astride his mule was a warming thing to see. One would surely credit him with enterprises of a most gleaming order. But it was precisely here that many experienced really annoying misgivings: (for all did wish him well — no wonder!) But he *did* do rather. . . odd things.

63) ON, ON, ON

Tremendous trifles — *On, on, on* — and then? Whitepanther beside the milk pitcher — Trifling tremendousnesses —

A NIGHT SONG (64

It has been a long time getting here, your letter. The leaves are nearly gone from the trees now. Saw something today in a shop-window which I wanted very badly to buy for you. — No matter.

POEM XVII SCAPE

65) THE FARAWAY BALLAD

Bloodred are the fishes that sleep in the grove. Bloodred are their dreaming faces, bloodred the leaflike scale on their little hands. Soon will the maidens come to wake them, the lilylike maidens. . .

THE FARAWAY BALLAD (66

Milkwhite are the fishes that sleep in the grove. Milkwhite the dreamlike glow from their little breasts that are so cold. Soon will the masters come to wake them, the masters of the longlost. . . O soon will the masters come in their snow-sheeted robes. . .

67) THE FARAWAY BALLAD

Deathcolored are the fishes that sleep in the grove. Deathcolored the fishes. . .

THE FARAWAY BALLAD (68

O the color of life itself are the fishes that sleep in the grove! Lifecolored are their slowly opening eyes, lifecolored the twiglike unfolding of their gentle hands! Soon they will come among us.

69) A NIGHT SONG

Each step down the lane to the mailbox is a kind of hell. There in the morning. . . *the sun. . . the birds singing all around me. . . everything green and clean-looking. . .* No letter from you. — From anyone.

FRIEND THE RABBIT (70

I like to think of him as he looked in his new suit of orange and white checks and pink velvet lapels. Hurrying along, whistling cheerfully, his mule having a smart time keeping pace. A gigantic sunflower behind either ear, a flaming red hat perched well back on his head. Hawking select unburial plots.

71) A NIGHT SONG

You once asked me what I wanted out of life. . . Let's say — No matter.

FRIEND THE RABBIT (72

They were both frowning up at the Tower Room, where sometimes lovely maidens have a hard deal escaping the clutches of wicked (but rich) kings. He whispered something to his mule, and — bam! ! ! no castle.

POEM XIX SCAPE

73) CONVERSATION WITH MIRRORS

"I don't always come off. . . umm, even second best." — "But you do have a fancy of yourself walking? I mean, when you *are* walking, not just sitting, or, perhaps, even, well, reclining." — "You didn't mention *running*. . . "

CONVERSATION WITH MIRRORS (74

"I was sure they'd bring it with them." — "For the sake of argument, what difference does that make? Your house is jammed to overflowing with stuff like that now." — "I even phoned them about it. Got them up out of bed." — "For the sake of argument, who cares!" — "Next time maybe I'll know better."

75) THE LATE AFTERNOON

A shadow falls across the table. . . drinks slowly of a cup, nibbles the roseleaf. . .

SUBSTANCE OF SHADOW (76

And when a thousand years have passed. . . Ah. Ah, yes. Shadowy figures of the little earth. . . Appointments which will not wait, which must be kept. Ah. Ah, yes. The worm at the heart of the roseleaf.

POEM XX SCAPE

77) THE HEART'S UNDERSTANDING

Above all I wish you joy in the things which are fashioned for joy, and an honest sorrow in what is of its nature sorrowful. Joy and sorrow — each is beautiful, and beautiful the heart's understanding of them.

THE BALANCE SHEET (78

Of all things save the doings of the heart, of a generous, unpossessing, free heart, ample to its own inclinations and needless of every other, when a life is at an end, O, of all things save this alone, what remains? What remains save those moments when heart wept, or when it burst in gladness. . ?

79) DUST'S ONLY ENEMY

A good and gentle heart. . . In this world there is nothing more beautiful.

WONDER REMAINS WONDER (80

There is in each life a quality, a special fragrance of the bone and of the flesh, individual, unmistakeable, exactly as it issued from the spirit's mold. A quality which nothing can in any manner alter.

POEM XXI SCAPE

81) MORE FABULOUS ANIMALS

This one may best be described as a "translation" — sort of a "brought-over." Think of a hallway made of wish-sponges, of a fruit tasting of street-cries: put them together, gingerly, tenderly — "add" *memories.* . .

THE LITTLE ESSAYS (82

Is Tomorrow Here? Of course. Tomorrow was a cooked goose from the moment it commenced to flash back a few of its least appetizing skills. Everyone saw them as "Progress" — Yes, chucking tomorrow's kitbag into the soup before anybody got round to caring what kind of soup would be a sensible soup to have.

83) CONVERSATION WITH MIRRORS

"For the sake of argument, suppose a revelation." — "Define your terms." — "From despair alone. . . "

NONESSENTIALISM IN PRACTICE (84

It's nonessential: 1) to believe; 2) to believe in believing; 3) to believe in believing in believing; 4) to believe in not believing; 5) to believe in not believing in believing; 6) to believe in not believing in believing in not believing.

POEM **XXII** SCAPE

85) A DIFFICULT UNDERTAKING

This day of life, to render some unimportantness beautiful.
Without "effort," "thought," or "cunning," to do that; and to
leave it — whether "gesture," "look," or "touching" — intact and
untarnished in its ordained place. What an undertaking!

NONESSENTIALISM IN PRACTICE (86

It's nonessential: 7) to recognize the inescapable poignancy
of the world, and all that takes place in it; one has only to make
"a brave effort" to discover "one's own true, *personal* set of
'values' "— through an "objective and sound, unflinching ap-
praisal of 'things as they *really* are.' " This should do the trick
very nicely.

87) THE FARAWAY BALLAD

Soulless; cold are the fishes that sleep in the grove. Soulless;
cold the fishes!

THE WORST SIN (88

Tonight, so quietly. . . *To offer something which the heart has
colored and made its own.* I am constantly amazed at how arrogant
people are; in the wonders and mysteries of this world, not to be
humble!

POEM XXIII SCAPE

89) GLAD ABOUT ANIMALS

I am glad about animals, about their many different kinds and appearances. I find it a pleasure to look at them, wonder about them, to wonder what they wonder about me. Wonderful comicals of their kind; of mine.

GLAD ABOUT FISHES&BIRDS (90

I am glad about the eagerplacid way they accept the miracle of themselves. It's marvelous the way they manneroffactly set about the business of gathering horsetailhairs for their nests and zoom-diving up over waterfalls and all the rest of it. Angels haven't it half over them! *What respect they have for their own methods.*

91) GLAD ABOUT SNAKES&SCORPIONS

I am glad about all the crawling things; their strange — and ever grace-filled — dignities.

GLAD ABOUT SEA&SKY (92

I am glad about this ever-changing and ever-renewing marriage — which seems to be celebrated more out of this world than in it. Glad of that watching blueness — which always disconcerts the more it reassures.

93) THE MODERN SICKNESS

On every hand there is a nasty slyness, a petty viciousness; not to serve any purpose really, just out of sheer inner spite — a nasty, vicious slyness. A nothing-for-nothing affair; petty, nasty, vicious — a sort of vegetarian cannibalism.

AN "HONEST" POLITICIAN (94

Himself he hired to speak at a dinner in his honor. All went well except anybody else could have hoked up something to say for him: he could think of nothing. "This unregenerate heel" is how he started; then he lapsed into censure of the most telling kind; and concluded, "But now, all flattery aside — "

95) BEWARE THE HARVEST

A petty, nasty, for-the-hell-of-it slyness is deliberately fash-ioned forth as "the modern mode." Look about you!

CONVERSATION WITH MIRRORS (96

"You. . . you make no effort to appreciate another point of view. You. . . errr. . . " — "How odd that you find your own tolerable. I find it detestable." — "You. . . you won't— just *willfully* won't see that. . . that. . . errr . . . " — "Oh, come now."

POEM **XXV** SCAPE

97) PORTRAITS ON WATER

Behold, then, this Old Grandfather Thing. A sneering, tired dull-green coat; high collar like an albino wolf's lips; the face shadowed over with little filths of petulant selfishnesses; in sum, a worthless, dirty, grayly decaying baby. Ah, flow swiftly. . .

SCENES OF CHILDHOOD (98

The air is striped like a circus tent; yellow, red, green. A great horse with golden mane is nubbling the tops of barns and steeples. Lovely in the tall grass. . . lying breathless and naked under the hot tent. . . Blowing locks of bushes, king's robe-crimson jewels flashing in the warm, silken spray. . . O caressing hands of the goddess. . ! !

99) I AM THE

Golden Browed Lion of the Waters. Come! *my gentle curls, sir; my cruelkind hands, m'lady.*

OTELLME'S AND WHEREDO'S (100

O tell me how I may clean my heart for the touching of such loveliness! Where do the cold gems sparkling there in the soft, purple curls of the meadow go to be reset and polished?

101) OTELLME'S AND WHEREDO'S

O tell me when the small lips of birds are at their bitter weeping in the wood, how shall I find tongue for the sorrow that's in me? Where do the sweet powers of the hushed heart gather?

I AM THE (102

King Who Disdains All Kingdoms, greater than the rending frost at the heart of a winter tree, less than the foam on the sea-bird's wing. I am the King Who Consumes All Kingdoms, mightier than the sea's voice under a north wind, far more affrighted than the break-breath prayer of a man dying.

103) SCENES OF CHILDHOOD

The hands of the old horse are picking withered, tired steps off the road.

PORTRAITS ON WATER (104

Behold, then, the Faithful One. Her breasts are wrinkled and shrunken now, like lumps of charred dough. Years, years of a life, they are there on her face as clawmarks; the beast has been at her — she is burnt dry under him. The sacred writing, the writing that tells of life's closing age. . . and of death's opening youth.

POEM **XXVII** SCAPE

105) SCENES OF CHILDHOOD

They gave us many little princesses to play with. Often three or four a day. And all of them enchanted. We did all sorts of jolly-dance things to wake them up. But they'd go away. Damn.

PORTRAITS ON WATER (106

Behold, then, the Sleeping Child. Arms folded around a glass-box which holds all the capital D's in the world. They shimmer and dance in the moonlight. One of them comes to rest on her mouth; another on her throat. . . Now the ugliest D of all — dark, dark. . . like a toaddog — it squats watching on her inno-cent forehead. . . watching all the others go away.

107) OTELLME'S AND WHEREDO'S

O tell me of the Hill of Waking Sleep! Where do the silent sing. . . ?

I AM THE (108

Long Cold House of Unending Sleep. Pale stainless hounds stand eternal guard that no errant sound or unwanted incitement mar the slumber of my guests. Plan to stay the night here; its peace is quite contagious.

109) I AM THE

Joy of the Desiring Flesh. The days of my living are summer days; the nights of my glory outshine the blazing wave-caps of the heavens at their floodtide! Mine is the confident hand shaping this world.

OTELLME'S AND WHEREDO'S (110

O tell me have you ever rounded the little curve-end of the land where the hills are like lovers parting in the woeful fret and press of the surf as it thunders upon the rocks with their graybrown toes like a giant's. . . and it and them as children crying for boats lost on a pond? Where do the severed of living go for their healing. . . ?

111) PORTRAITS ON WATER

Behold, then, the Ancient Queen. Summer cringes at her fingers' ends. . . their wiltingcold spreading everywhere.

SCENES OF CHILDHOOD (112

Prudence drank of the moonhoney spilling upon the lawn; Caution got smashed under the tread of an appleblossom; Manly Reserve was carried off on the saddle of a junebug; Proper Respect for Elders succumbed in the process of a becoming that was more like a begoing. But bless them and me.

113) KINDNESS OF CLOWNS

But if houses are many things to many people, they can be even fewer things to fewer people. And clowns, being always fewer — because nicer — than anybody, a house less than one to them becomes "*FORALL.*"

MY JOURNEY'S JOURNEYING (114

Might I have been your Inn beyond this brief night-place's stopping — O spirit, poor guest, sinking down at the woodsedge in this great dark where all lives are hidden. Might I have been a voice speaking back from the realm of what has not yet been, I would have told you not to come!

115) KINDNESS OF CLOWNS

Suspicion made the first pairapants; but, Joey, it'll be love'll take off the last.

CONVERSATION WITH MIRRORS (116

"Why do you suppose they keep moving the candles from one window to the other?" — "To show that there's something doing inside there." — "Something doing?" — "Yes, something doing. Like showing you where the dark is sparklingest!"

POEM XXX SCAPE

117) GOLDEN PLUM BUDS

We imagine one another so badly. We confuse one another with appearances that form in chairs and oceanliners and with being some longago-Greek or "young girl walking across field at sevenpm April3rd" or being "mykeeper'sbrother."

GOLDEN PLUM BUDS (118

Whatever we imagine for one another is wrong to the extent that we separate a state of being from its doesness. Because all appearances have a common origin in the unseeable fluidity *which issues forth from the action of its own flowing.* Existence is verb. (No "objects," no "things-to-be-named"— *doing itself does itself do.*)

119) MY INNOCENT COMPANIONS

They imagine an earth, a sky; imagine that they are alive: and they die.

FRIEND THE RABBIT (120

He imagines himself a bird with long ears, ball-y tail, chassis lovingly covered with soft golden fur. At sea a fortnight he sights a ship, but everybody a-bored pretends to see only a flying rabbit.

POEM **XXXI** SCAPE

121) MORE FABULOUS ANIMALS

The "being a twig in a child's hand" animal has intent and lovely eyes. (Do you, even now, O rose-hued silhouette, imagine a moment when life can permit its gaze to wander from the "unseen"?)

WHERE IS EVERYONE? (122

If you say pardon it won't matter. If you say sorry-sorry it won't get you covered with no godhair. If you say I am a nicer place than where I am it won't get you overlapped with the Princess of the Submerged Pyramid. But if you say beautifulbeautifulmoon they'll lower the boom!

123) MORE FABULOUS ANIMALS

The "being something distant and striding" animal won't bequeath you any Gospels For Gallowsbait.

WHERE IS EVERYONE? (124

If you say nodice it won't genuinate. If you say gitoutaherejack it won't do them no droop. If you say I don't fit me nomore it won't splug. But if you say hurrahhurraheverybody then watch out!

119

POEM **XXXII** SCAPE

125) A NIGHT SONG

You letter makes me think of two eyes, very beautiful, very thoughtful, but somehow. . . *only* eyes — I mean there's no face to go with them! Oh, it's not what you think — nothing *that* simple. No matter.

VISIT AMONG TREES (126

So that's why I have come here: some part of me has demanded that I come. That's why I may not explain it now — at least until I am less clear about it. Other parts of me are waiting in other undamaged places — waiting to be sorted, assembled, identified: they will tell me when.

127) VISIT AMONG TREES

Garden us in this loneliness of outer selves — O eyes of what we see!

A NIGHT SONG (128

I am not interested in any of that: you may believe what you like. The detail of the whole, there's all and enough generality to last me a while. Begging the issue? Yep, on my knees!

POEM **XXXIII** SCAPE

129) A NIGHT SONG

No, it's not just to be another make-damn funny onion with legs, piddling up his little puddle of "opinions" and "moral convictions" so that some even worse fool may be tempted over for a sniff. . .

A NIGHT SONG (130

I am glad you like the other version, but suspect someone of priming your lag in the matter of those "tied boxes." You do have your hushed side: not to be spooky about it, all compliments are troubling — when they're not just longgeorged tiresome. Of course everyone is serious; that's what's so dam BSquarish!

131) A NIGHT SONG

And flies *also* are thicker than water. "Overtones of psycho-pathological intensity." — "Pa-llease! not *that* chickenchat!"

THE POLEMIST'S COW (132

Avec are clover 'n butterclups this other one, a Dog that up to me in unambiguous haste arrives; who am I? some private-gabbed Pericles warming his rostrum with ept albeit provincial supplications? — Friar Middenstomp, open that beer!

133) THE ONLY DOG

Which was a Cat soon found that to follow the fashion of his kind he must leg it round the rascals while yet the Sun and the Moon and the Pretty Dandelion were in respectful accord.

THE ONLY DEARLITTLEOWL (134

Which was an Allblack Polar Bear fell down some water. O what's the worry, he could still be pinning them up. He could still be running the ole horn in under the wallpaper. So! in full stride! away and alas, for Jesus and the little dimpled angels whose bags are all safely checked 'n counted.

135) WHERE IS EVERYONE?

If you say Godnods they won't bootyer. But if you say damnoodlewits oh brother!

THE ONLY GREATLION (136

Which was a Parttime Clock began to cling outside a little because you will be well and you will be wondered O when on some other star all those second thoughts have time to get thunk.

POEM XXXV SCAPE

137) ANOTHER DAY GONE

This. . . and it is already that. On, on we go, baffled by the shadow of this In-Out; baffled to that point of cunning which declares: It is so little, it is nothing, it is enough.

NONESSENTIALISM IN PRACTICE (138

It's nonessential to believe that the special quality of every life resides not in its being (if by being we mean being *somewhere:* and if we don't, whose else's tail shall we chase?), but in its strange motionability, its headlong flight from anything and everything that even remotely smacks of "this day", "this place".

139) NONESSENTIALISM IN PRACTICE

It's nonessential to reject all "dayness"; thought is of what "is". — (But *where's* "thought"?)

KINDNESS OF CLOWNS (140

So all was a day! We planted the rosebush as a sign of peace between our leagues. Cheer up, lad; your arguments sound like do but smell like don't — so, let's spit us some fatter hares.

141) THE LITTLE ESSAYS

What Is Right? Much depends on whether you want to grow nettles or clover: on whether you've come to applaud or just to swipe clothes off the line; on whether you bring a halter or a head-dress.

THE ONLY HEN (142

Which was a Butterfly had to cross the ocean five times before she could get a shirtwaist that halfway suited; and even then she didn't think the back quite bonny enough — so she put it in front and sat on it until everybody had gone home. Then she fetched out a bottle and got skyeyed.

143) FRIEND THE RABBIT

He came dancing in and presented her with a child asleep on a leaf.

I AM THE (144

One Who Sits Watching You. Without feeling that there is too much at stake; without feeling that it really matters very much what becomes of you. — What goes on inside that leaf is more important anyway.

145) BRIGHT *OMBRES CHINOIS*

Because something here does not enchant, are those little stars, so brilliant! so abiding! to be accounted faults of a like unlording . . . the Tale allow no child ever again to say, "Look! whose eyes are those?"

ALL ARE ANIMALS (146

You know that trees are animals like any others; just as flowers and lakes — and even what we think and what we say, what we dream, what we imagine — these too are animals, animals like any others. And stars, and sky, the moon, the sun, the earth — oh, yes, these too! all are animals!

147) BRIGHT *OMBRES CHINOIS*

The animal of sleep — ah, within this one we pass our lives; until suddenly. . . !

POOR PUCCIO D'ANIELLO (148

Oh, come along, admit it! On Monday we shall what, on Tuesday we shall not, on Wednesday we shall rot — which leaves the rest of the week for counting blessings. Ah, we are the fortunate vegetables!

POEM XXXVIII SCAPE

149) FLIES HAVE FINGERS

With which they hold their food. Just as any paulr duke phutz-ing around the carbarn in hopes of making an impression on the motorman's daughter, who sometimes at late afternoon has been known to peek in.

FLIES HAVE FINGERS (150

"Ah, dear maryanne lowder, howdydo, howdydo, gel; my heart it is napoleon-shaped — why, even my ears and teeth they be like that bloody elf's!" But it's only a machinist back to check over the switchbox into which some small boys yesterday jammed a riflebutt. "Howdydo, yerself! n'stop gnawin on thet gawddum wheel!"

151) FLIES HAVE FINGERS

With which they don't sign treaties. Or write speeches. Or applaud ulyssesqnuisances.

FLIES HAVE FINGERS (152

And the feet of the air, toes; but what is maryanne lowder doing off in yonder ballpark with jackb handy, the oily machinist? — And out of all the all. . . apes'n meadowlarks, meat, bread, cornlikker'n anewmoon!

POEM **XXXIX** SCAPE

153) COMMENTS FOR STRINGEDHORNS

You say, Let them have it, and I don't know whether you mean, Let them have it, or, Let them have it; whether you hanker to join or disjoint these intellectual pimps, liberal punks, and college-poetiquettes.

COMMENTS FOR STRINGEDHORNS (154

I once thought that if people got a good whiff of what is really with all these lying, swindling, sanctimonious Democracy-pushers, they'd make some kind of instinctive grab for the flush; but I'masonofagun! it's worth your neck keeping out of their way as they come charging hellbent right up to the bowl's edge!

155) A NIGHT SONG

Your letter must have pleased you to write: it's so beautifully, so *seriously* petty.

A NIGHT SONG (156

No, I don't care to go on with the "Comments." Let the swine have their green-frothed swill. Shlup! Shlup! Only let them hurry it. Meantime, — oh, I almost forgot to thank you for the books!

POEM **XL** SCAPE

157) APRIL 6, 1956

The day begins in the morning. You get your pants and shirt on, open the door, a man says, "OK, just pay me half now, you'll get the rest of your horse later; here's the bridle."

APRIL 6, 1956 (158

Around Noon the afternoon begins. You put the franks'n friedbeans on the plate, man walks in leading a green duck on a string. "Your horse likes the company of a duck, but your only charge is for the gold chain." — "What gold chain?" — "The one your duck swallowed. D'you think they come that color!"

159) APRIL 6, 1956

(O little duck, why d'you keep edging up to that damn telephone? It's disconnected.)

APRIL 6, 1956 (160

Sundown. . . You set bottles'n glasses out, man walks in with two long goofy paper ears stuck to his hatband, does a pile on the floor, says, "You weren't expecting a *real* horse for that price, were you?"

POEM XLI SCAPE

161) THIS BEWILDERING HOUSE

All of us are at the window, looking out of this strange room; men. . . whose skins on one side are black, are yellow, are brown, are white, are red — standing close together in this bewildering house.

WHAT FANTASTIC CREATURES! (162

I look out of this window — that is what it is like there, for all who look out of windows, from apartments, from farmhouses, from churches, jails, schoolrooms, cityhalls: the sky and a street, fields, bridges, waterfalls. . . my God! these are all such *strange* things! and those "people" moving there, what extraordinarily fantastic creatures!

163) BARNS, SALOONS, BROTHELS

Who'd care for a glimpse of these things *turned to flesh*. . . and staring back!

IN MOMENTARY ETERNITY (164

O bluebell my brother! Tiger! sparrow! moon! and snowflake too! O great brothers! One little one of us looks out of me—but O how many, many of me are looking out of you, dear brothers!

129

POEM **XLII** SCAPE

165) WITH THIS ROSE

I thee wake. And in this room — yes, to become preoccupied
with . . . oh, I don't know, let's say, God's digestion, one must
be convinced that nearer matters aren't worth too much: *responsi-
bilities, mysteries, devotions, are here.*

ALGO Ó NADA (166

Truth must in. We are the work. The made-world is all decora-
tion, and only matters that when it is not completely given over to
its appointed task of providing a setting of the most consummate
brutality, sterility, and hideousness, it is just plain ridiculously
silly! Look about you — those clothes, houses, cars — woweee! !

167) YOU'RE ALL NUTS

Boobs, scamps, frauds, and all you assorted blaugh-swilling
drearies — oh, COME OFF IT!

SUNDAY, APRIL 8th (168

With this rose I thee world. Fashioned in Love, its color the
color of heart'sblood! See, though its leaves do wilt and fall, yet
is it rose; and never any mean or sullied thing. Wonder it!

A Letter to God

A Letter to God

the wing is burning wing is burning O burn the wing for the
wing is burning

My heart is not in the things here.

Men have made no effort to live by your word or by the word of
any Good. This has angered me always. Childhood had not the color
of the beautiful but of poverty and learning to kill what was best to
know and love or be. So I write out of an awkward shyness; not
understanding the angel. And the way to be near you I understand
not. And the methods of love and joy and light are not understood.
Nor of hate and pain and fear is there any manner or need not known.

This black village. Houses, a lake and . . . *(eye of fire O the Eye
is on fire)*   gray loose frog
squatting on the arms of the Cross

I first went to school in a town of steel. The boys had faces like
thin cats—the geography of evil; the history of monsters—I want to
remind you that I understand little in your sense. Sometimes I pick
up a stone in the street, and just hold it in my hand. That may have
nothing to do with present difficulties in the world; but it gives me
pleasure and can cause no ultimate harm to anyone. I was fifteen
before I got all of myself in. Until then I seemed to smile when I felt
angry, grit my teeth together when expected to talk. My clothes never
pleased me in color or in the way they felt when I took them off at

night. They were like the skin of an animal I knew nothing about. The same with my teeth: often they were cold and felt too sharp in my mouth.

1915: Yellow snow in Cleveland. Lame woman swinging a rope.

1922: To kill of course: "Don't stare at me!"

1923: And the flesh was made a ward.

1928: Her crying made me cry. Moved to new hungers. Like nosebleed.

1931: And the Church . . . glittering throats in a gray choir.

1934: It is not always easy to live a good life.

Water is cruel water is cold kind water deep sweet water O then let me be quiet and quiet and still. For stranger stronger art thou.

"Do you hate me?"
"I know thee not—not even in fear."

Black tree . . . rust run house of darkness lake of evil
        cabin terrible wren spool grin MILK leaf light
scrubwoman dip your mop in the skittering pail of heaven
merchant sell on the playful blood of untroubling boys, *you snake!*
king put your sword to the land of light and land the great fish
You God tame
O make tame what men call war
but is the only condition of their 'peace'

O loud sing the leaving lark

Yesterday I tried to remember the first time I ever tasted an apple. Then I thought of this letter to you and it seemed an unimportant thing to know. . .

134

But I'm not sure.

Certainly your patterns are bigger than mine. And . . .

Why don't you come down and carry on your fight? What exactly did you mean when you said

"Thou shalt not kill."?

Come down God and continue your fight against this pious murder. —"Under certain circumstances; in order to properly defend; in event that no other method of survival is forthcoming"—

NO

"Thou shalt not kill."

And what right has anyone to make people think you were a liar.

My father used to say that I looked too long at people. It is true that they suspected me of not understanding them, and this made them want to make me uneasy; which they did by gripping my shoulder or by turning suddenly away.

November 16, 1939: I am first conscious of another being in myself.

Banners

hoofs (O the swift graceful target)

a wound perhaps

I question not your authority.

Nor my own.

I make preparation to use them.

Has lived. Loves. In the world!

Just as there is no end to joy in life . . . an existence resembling every beautiful. Cry not. Be not mean. Do not cheat. Make no money out of blood. Believe in man. Belief in man is God.

the use of guilt is death

People look out of the holes in their eyes.
The eye itself is of the spirit.
Not to see, but seeing.

O an inch from the rosebush or a thousand miles from this
murder . . . this being here!
Ghost, ghost upon the sea, have you tidings?
have you angels found?
O a tiny place away from the world where we may lie,
my love and me?
        Blockhead!
Dear God, I don't want to go to bed tonight. There should be a
lock on what I have to think.

December 5, 1939: Visited by a man and woman from another
world.
December 7, 1939: Wilbur (you would like him) broke a piece
out of a poem by One of the Lads (can never tell them apart) and
used it as the headstone for a gnat he had got fond of.
December 8, 1939: Spent the day filing a complaint against the
U.S. Senate. Rather pleased to know I have a say in matters per-
taining to.
December 9, 1939: Walked down Cornelia Street. Met nobody
I knew nor did anyone else.
December 14, 1942: Planning a little surprise for my enemies.
More about this anon, I reckon.

August 13, 1943: Wilbur and I discussed the policy of Our State Dept. To be sure. And How. You said it.

I have no children because I couldn't feed them. My wife never has a new coat and I may have to write novels. So do I do. It is a situation I wish you'd do something about because nobody else gives a damn. I can't take the rich. Means two things.

(How do you like this?)
The cave was lined with blue fur. A princess sat near the entrance, and in her hand she hald a chalice made of gold. She drank of the wine and softly died.

Far away, almost to the end of the most distant land, her lover paused at his task of creating a new being.

Two things walked through the shadow which like a woolen shawl hung on the shoulders of the air. Their faces were streaked with yellow chalk and a single horn grew out of their foreheads. It was night when they reached the cave.

They did not touch her. They moved to a corner away from the world, and, lowering their beautiful, sad heads, wept.

(And this?)
No one supposed the chaining of that particular beast to a tree would bring the world to an unsightly end. Nor did it. But it did effect a curious condition in the lives of three people who had their home a score of miles out at sea.

It was the howling.

It was a sense on the air that terror had a face which could be seen. And feet really which walked in search of open graves.

The three were John Jefferson.

They had been so named by a wave which took them to mother. One was tall with box-deep eyes. One was fair, slim-skulled and strong as thrice-heated tea. The third was almost a Christ—he. . .
O John Jefferson!
What will become of thee?
O what, what will become of thee?

To be whole!
—how we hunger to be clean!
—these dazzling messengers from white suns—
Is it possible to
You smile, God

November 16, 1941: "It's going to snow soon," I said.
I ruffled her hair as she set the table. She crumpled back the bread-wrapper and cut five slices. I pulled up the chairs. The cat rubbed against my legs as we sat down. Suddenly we both laughed and I got up and went around to kiss her. She pushed me away and made a crinkly face. "Eat, you big silly," she said; but she sprang to her feet and pressed her body hard against mine. Holding her in my arms with a savage joy, I glanced out of the window:
"Ah Christ! will you just look at it snow," I said.

They moved into the circle
which a snail had drawn
on the forehead of a weeping lion

This marble casket. *O laughing maiden* . . .
war perhaps. Be not unwary, God. The war
draws no circle

. . . .

Killed in action,
Sept. 24, 1945

You know as well as I do
that . . .

It is without doubt unfortunate that the truly beautiful part was
destroyed before anyone could see it. I know I would now like much
to have even the dimmest knowledge of its perfections.

Whatever your hidden motives were, there does seem to have
been shown a tragic carelessness in the manner of the defilement.
Something else surely could have been done with us—even at the
final moment—even in the white hour of your agony when you
regretted your lowly creation, might not some smallest vestige of
mercy have been spared . . ?

I am not able to say how exactly it would have altered my
holdings, but I am not far off believing a dog might better have been
commissioned to the endeavors I have before me.

I think of the girl I loved when I was twelve. I think of the
thousands of eyes and voices that have gone through her since then.
Perhaps she is dead. . .

I think of the creek I used to walk along coming from school.
Of the teacher who shot himself in front of the solid geometry class.
Of the time I said a lively Anglo-Saxon word by mistake in assem-
bly. . .

I think of my father being carried home with half his foot cut off in the mill. I think of my brother driving around town in a low-slung, tan racing car he picked up in a junkyard for sixteen bucks. Of my uncle stumbling into High Mass drunk as a lord and undressing at the altar. . . .

What are you thinking of at this moment, God?

I cannot really expect the old man to take his feet out of the river and make a saddle for a horse nobody would want to ride anyway.

He looks up and winks at me as I go tearing by with some plan or other to stop everybody from running straight on to hell.

Perhaps he understands in the way he has always understood the things which at all concern him.

But it never seriously appeals to him to take his feet out of the gently flowing water.

May 27, 1942: I have seen the new being.

Aside to your daughter Keela:

I am not permitted to speak to you when the white leopard is in the room. On the evening of Peretho (Jan. 6 in heaven) you will walk under the lemon trees which your father planted. You will wear the pink dress with the margarineflies on the collar. Do not grow bitter if I do not always accompany you to market. The eyes of the geese in their paper crates look with too much pity upon us. Perhaps the wan leopard will not come today . . . say, how is this? The blood will have dried on his paws by the time our true representation to the Other One can be made—

May 28, 1942: The light is blinding.

In runaway order

out of the green life

O ALL IN FIRE

mother

Some useless fellow. My cold rule, on nineth hill. . .
every murder is the murder of Thee

as I everliving lean in love up to that bright tree

Silence then!
"This day is death's."
Red full sweet beast.

"What time is it in the tiger's garden?"
You damned cheats eating your kill—
Bloody handed pigs
Defying Thy announced will
    It is hard to have friends now. People are going to pieces too
fast. They hate anyone who does not bleed fog and sickness.
    I watch the young men go. Nothing can heal them.
    Death won't. These are machine-made . . . not meant to feel or
to think—
    What have you told them, God, that they go thus to slay and to
be slain—
WHAT HAS ANYONE TOLD THEM?

May 29, 1942: All I am ever kind to—
    "Wear the shawl His mother made."
    "I've given it away."
    "Given it away . . ?"
    "Yes—To the one of evil."

Then for the good!

Blackness in the mouth of their walking. Is it profitable to be
merciful . . . Joy, moon, *moon*—"Long ago the world rode away
from the village of my father."—white cold towers
(valley of unreturning faith)
Here they sleep.
Who know Thee not. The bed (in blood), under low
stars
"Do not die."
Standing in their salt sweat . . . hairy mouths full of a speech no man
anywhere has belief in. Big plans gone west.
These do not want Thee. Except for fun. To paint flags on Your
belly.
To make war right.

All is a lie in their world.

God, your noble little sons are mad.
They breathe murder.
Their eyes steam.
The dimout of death.
This day is his.
Now is his hurry.
More than dying, nothing is done.
But as toads drinking snot.

Cloud over me this cry, this togethering of a last darkness—
I think your noble little sons are
thieves and cutthroats
stewing in their mess   Go low Light.
fouling the pants of an idiot   Build a throne.

STAR

And the horizon of love was the morning of the 8th day.

Ah, the hogwild jades of murder neigh. . .

I order you to destroy them.
I am tired of their dirt.
We have a right to live!
None shall kill when all are comforted.
Give us the earth now.
Give us the peace now.
Give us the daily bread now.
O give us the land and the creatures of the field and the silent
beautiful wood
that we may feed and shelter
all men equally
for man's only duty is to man.

God, we shall accept the terms of your world.
That we may not kill.
That we may not hate.
That the things of labor belong to all men.
That the things of spirit live in all men.
That the things of God are on earth for the use of all men.

None shall kill when all are completed.
None shall hate when all are at love.

August, 1943.

HURRAH FOR ANYTHING

W H E R E ?

There's a place the man always say
Come in here, child
No cause you should weep
Wolf never catch the rabbit
Golden hair never turn white with grief
Come in here, child
No cause you should moan
Brother never hurt his brother
Nobody here ever wander without a home
There must be some such place somewhere
But I never heard of it

NEVER LIKE THIS
BACK IN MARBLEHEAD

For the bed went to bed
And the chair sat down
Now that was rude, sirs
No way for gents to act
The parlor floor paced back and forth
The wallpaper reached
Out a rosy fist
And almost decabbaged grandma
You kids think that's proper
Oh, oh, here comes a hungry-looking potroast
That blur was just me coming back for my clothes

148

BRINGING HOME
THE LITTLE BRIDE

Ah! just beyond that next native hut . .
See! there's somebody waving now!
Oh you'll like my family . .
They're an easy ridin' bunch.
One time my old dad just stood
In. one place
Until his suspenders rotted . .
Got himself jailed for disturbing the peace.
Hi there, Buckets! — she's my ma —
Meet Abbybelle . . No, she's *not* got round legs!
This here bit of jazz is called an automobile, stupid!

THE PEACEFUL LIER

I used to flit about hoping
To brush up
On what everybody
Said was so special.
Well, I saw the big shtoonks
Kicking the cans off
The little shtoonks — *and!* . .
Charging them for the service.
Now, I admit that's a pretty special setup,
But if you don't mind I think
I'll just lie this one out in my own way.

DON'T TELL ME

Want to be nice and kind
Don't tell me what happen
I saw a light up in the sky
Never knew they smoked cigars up there
I heard a noise off on the water
Since when the fishes start packin' guns
If you want to be kind and nice
Just don't tell me what's goin' on
I saw the Clean Man a-standin'
'Way up above the world
And what his eyes were wet from wasn't laughin'

WE MEET

We are every so often rustled
By something afar —
In this case, a stretch of watery coast
Along which saunter a Cow
Made of brilliant red roses,
And two heavily bearded schoolchildren;
And in the other, by something quite near —
That is, the imminent presence in us
Of certain vague and shadowy hungers,
Of dreams (and even painful rejoicings),
Which presumably add up to the same thing.

I AM TIMOTHY THE LION

I live in an old sour maple tree
With Happy Jake, who is
A small goldfish;
There is also a short-necked swan,
Two very base players, a bull still wrapped
In pink tissue paper, and a policeman
Shaped like a watering can;
But they're all afraid of sunstroke,
So me and Jake just sit out on our limb here
And shout *Bon Dieu! Bon Dieu!*
Every time the phone rings up in one of those clouds.

TRAVELERS OF NECESSITY

Well you see they spoke Hat and that
Meant if you so much as whispered "kettle"
Clang-bang went everybody's head
With the soup hanging down
Why once a forgetful old man happened
To remark that he'd badly like
To take him a bath
On a ferriswheel
Well now a couple hundred damn near drowned
Before somebody thought to say a common soldier word
Of course, they've had to be on the move ever since

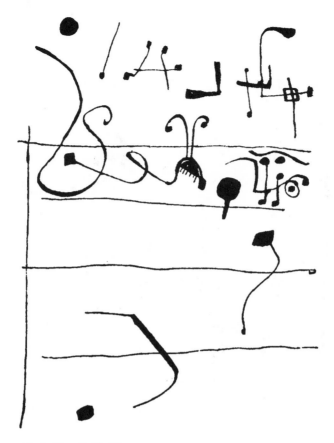

FAR OUT

But he took him down to the roof,
And the other old woman grabbed
Their dripping cigars and glowing tarbooshes
And fed them to the baby.
The Mayor rode by on a large-nosed trout —
It was snowing in his head.
Oh, what is the use of little yellow combs
If your train don't never come?
Oh, you can throw eighty-seven bricks
At any hour your honey ain't around,
It'll still seem as sad and as blank
As an eye that's buried in the ground.

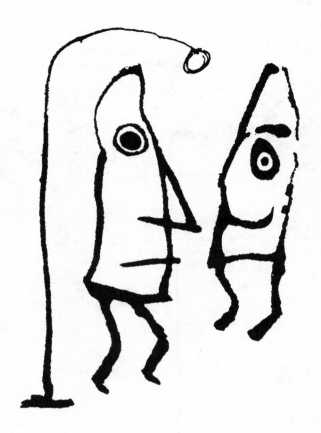

WHAT'S THIS I HEAR
ABOUT CHARLIE?

He'd just come out of his house, see;
Stopped to pull an arrow
Out of his leg . .
You know, since their mama took sick,
The boys put on little shows-like to amuse her,
Bullrun, the Custer bit, maybe a bear-shoot . .
So poor Charlie had just straightened up
When out of the corner of his eye
He sees this big grizzly in the doorway . .
Well, Charlie naturally thought it was one of his brothers —
The fatal power of suggestion, I guess you might call it.

O ! O !

I'm surprise so many eucalyptus tree
Ain't a chestnut.
Be almost more comfortable,
If they wanted to be one,
And nobody minded any.
Like you see so many tired little mule
Can't never be a dragonfly,
And stick his head in the water.
Unless they already are
What somebody else don't want to be,
Or vice versa.

I AM THE CHICKEN

My name is Harry and I like
Everybody; but as a smatter of lack,
There's nobody here, hardly . .
Only some green-cheeked squirrels, whom I fancy
Have lost their boatfares; and a wobbly gaited
Young mouse with a row of sputtering candles
On his back . . Only these, and a little baldheaded man
Who comes every Wednesday with a big shiny bucket
And chases me in and out of the thorny bushes —
Of course he is entitled to his own impression,
But do I have to look like a *cow*
Just because I like everybody!

IT IS THE HOUR

A sigh is little altered
Beside the slow oak;
As the rustling fingers
Of the sun
Stir through the silvery ash
That begins to collect on the forest floor.
It is the hour
When the day seems to die
In our arms;
And we have not done
Much that was beautiful.

WHEN IS A STALKER
NOT A STALKER

Like a downy feather
That floats up the shaft
Of some deserted mattress factory,
Where, during the lunch hour,
A sub-clerk with a weak chin
And a bad cold, phoned his mother
That he would be delayed getting home
Because he had to go see about getting a new radio tube,
And after that maybe stop and examine some clock-pattern
    socks
He'd noticed on sale, I go aimlessly on,
Not really knowing whether I'm running from somebody,
Or somebody's just chasing me because I'm running.

PERHAPS IT IS TIME

Does anyone think it's easy
To be a creature in this world?
To ask for reasons
When all reasons serve only
To make the darkness darker,
And to break the heart?
— Not only of man,
But of all breathing things?
Perhaps, friends, it is time
To take a stand
Against all this senseless hurt.

THE "GREATER GOOD"

Is usually standing near some peaceful tree ..
And may always be found lost
When it comes to "voting"
Or reading the newspapers;
For if he wanted to study up
To be a bloody nut,
He'd choose something more sensible —
Like sticking his head in a buzzsaw.
He's got a hole at either end of him,
Both of which he respects to the point
Of never confusing their functions.
("Governments etc" please copy.)

WHERE TRIBUTE IS DUE

What're you gonna do with people
What kind of eraser
You gonna use on them
Now the mistake's been made
What're you gonna do about it
If you burn them
The stink is bound to linger
Even on those holy-dollar curtains
You've set up to keep them apart
So you're probably right in just letting them die
Like you're doing now

PLAYERS IN LOW SEE

I just had me a talk with Bob Dog . .
He still got his big wobbly tongue hangin' out?
Yep, got him a nice little old lemon ranch now.
He always did want a bald head with hair on it.
You're still not doin' much to me, bub.
I was just thinking . . you know, I —
Sure, I know . .
Look at that damn sneery little sky!
Yeah . .
And all this goddam little — little —
Yeah. Well, be seein' yuh, big shot.

164

ONLY CHERRIES?

They didn't want me around
Said I couldn't have no cherries
Or watch them pick cherries
Or even stand near the table
Where one of those Kultur-Kookie-Klucks
With the big fat-legged smile
Was fixing to pop a nice red cherry
In on top of his gold spoon
You know I don't like those people
Who act as if a cherry
Was something they'd personally thought up

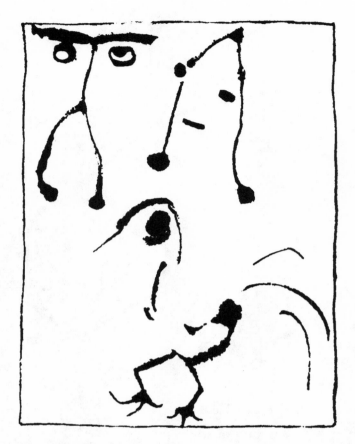

FLAP*ja*CKS ON THE PIA*zz*A

When Keravvo Jazell invented the "Conductor"
There were still no streetcars or *surging* trains
As we think we know them; instead, each
Householder would twine a bit of old piano wire
Around the bed at night — binding it
Tighter and tighter, until . . *wam! bam!*
The tracks thus made, however, had a tendency
To end in swamps, or up tall trees;
Moreover, many people took to sleeping
With the livestock — on those long winter nights!
In fact, in some more backward localities,
The ticket-seller must often have reckoned
The good Jazell to be not only the father of the baggagecar,
But of a whole new species to ride in it as well.

ALL THE ROARY NIGHT

It's dark out, Jack
The stations out there don't identify themselves
We're in it raw-blind, like burned rats
It's running out
All around us
The footprints of the beast, one nobody has any notion of
The white and vacant eyes
Of something above there
Something that doesn't know we exist
I smell heartbreak up there, Jack
A heartbreak at the center of things —
And in which we don't figure at all

167

ONE WHO HOPES

Born like a veritable living prince
With small, pink, rectangular feet
And a disposition to hair, I stand
Under the blazing moon and wonder
At the disappearance of all holy things
From this once so promising world;
And it does not much displease me
To be told that at seven tomorrow morning
An Angel of Justice will appear,
And that he will clean up people's messes for them —
Because if he is, and he does, he'll be more apt
To rub their lousy snouts in it.

HOW COME?

You ain't my brother now
I don't trust the way
You stamp your feet on me
I don't shine up
To this devil-goosin' stuff
You been layin' on in my behalf
Oh you ain't my lovin' buddy now
Sometime I think the manner
You come in my house
And dirty-arm me around
Is something I don't particularly cherish

WHO CAN TELL?

Does the resolute little hostler's apprentice
At his mid-morning lunch under a borrowed umbrella —
For who can tell when it may rain, or some overzealous
Pilot maybe drop a camshaft or a couple propeller nuts? —
Of meatloaf and unworked kraut sluiced down
With some overpriced 39-a-quart muscatel . .
Not to forget the wedge of gummy layercake
Which he had traded two excellent kumquats for —
I say, does he ever, in his very inmost self,
Softly murmur: Oh boy! there'll be plenty of snazzy stuff
For every one of us! *an' every man a whole goddam. parade
All by himself!* — Only, I keep forgetting to recall
Just how that's gonna come about . .

A RIDDLE FOR THE 1ST
OF THE MONTH

What has twenty tails and no rear?
What marks time in a haystack,
And yet would beat horseracing hollow?
What distrusts wet rope on principle,
And yet has a burning interest in hanging fire?
What blushes to see two new bikewheels in a rut,
And yet madly yanks at the drawers of old dressers?
What puts a good face on always getting the short end,
And yet saves the real lip-smacking for the fattest?
If you can answer these things, and send me fifty,
We'll both have a lot less to worry about.

A MORNING IN BIC-BIC..
IN THE GOOD OLD DAYS

Here outside meadow'n moorlet, the goosetooth
Dawn waits by the chipped pink zinc sink;
Waits for Samallyn, who is there, to yearn
Roguishly up the masked trash-treader's funnel:
"Hustle, Mikeleen, you darkish bit of muscled fluff!
The haroohs are again gathering in the nectarish sloobery.
Oh, I tell yuh . . plenty a times I — "
It wercles loosely past the steaming peach-butter vats;
Musses with only scarcely an inaudible clack through
The long gruff shepherd's sister-in-law's youngest daughter's
Sparklingly vague collection of flea circus trapeze miniatures.

NEWS FROM BACK OF YONDER

They ran into the lumber room,
But Tom, whose name was Rodney,
Couldn't make it; so, pushing
Out to the road again, she met
Her mother for the first time,
And an apple blinking to and fro
On a sort of hair, from which
Nothing grew except a tobogganslide.
Wow! soon the lawnchairs will be ripe —
There! feel *those* delicate little ribs!
Ah, nothing quite so pretty as the chest
Of a steaming bowl of tomato soup!

DOGS BOATING

Stroll out the Krinnzer "hoop".
The president of shuffles can wait.
Bind on & brink this woundy mess.
We shoved & shrived them cold plagetts.
At the beginning no kagging was only so.
May it equal if some are out?
Oh no . . Beg under the hands.
There are no stupid births. That's the jat.
Oh that's really drained it, Sally!
And to Then. And to little flutes: (*next*) . .
Him where no turning sifts in soon & jat's no-Jat.

I WENT TO THE CITY

And there I did weep,
Men a-crowin' like asses,
And livin' like sheep.
Oh, can't hold the han' of my love!
Can't hold her little white han'!
Yes, I went to the city,
And there I did bitterly cry,
Men out of touch with the earth,
And with never a glance at the sky.
Oh, can't hold the han' of my love!
Can't hold her pure little han'!

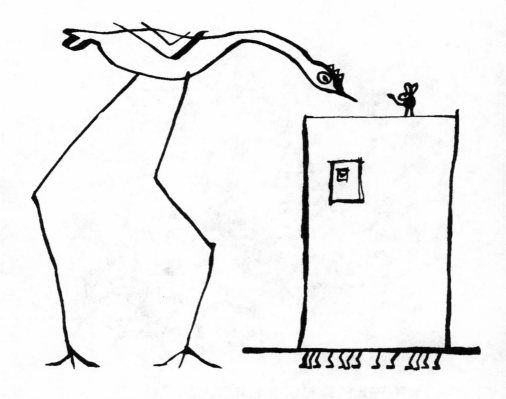

A WORD TO THE SUFFICIENT

Won't do you no good, Mr. Rabbit
Either you pays the rent
Or I perch my fist
On top your carrot-crusher
And quit that chasing through the mezzanine
At all hours
Telling everyone you've got
God's sister coming on a surprise visit
And you need say four or five bucks
For a cab out to the airport
Brother! what a mess you'll be in if she comes on the bus

YES, BLUEBELL, THIS TIME
IT IS GOODBYE

You better scatter
Head for that lonesome window
Ask the pretty lady
Please let us the hell in
'Cause it don't wash off
Poor bluebell's all covered with blood
Her little leaf don't look like a heart no more
Her little leaf look just like something
Some goddam maddog's been crappin' on
You better head out of here but fast

THE COWBOY
WHO WENT TO COLLEGE

There was a cowboy went to college,
Where somebody spilled ink on his horse.
He went to the dean in charge of such things
And was told that that gentleman
Had just popped out to the can again.
"Oh, he has, has he!" cried the cowboy;
"And me thinking it might be an accident —
"Why, hell, it's part of the damn curriculum!"

THE LITTLE MAN
WITH WOODEN HAIR

There was a little man with wooden hair
Who'd sneak into the rear of buses
And holler, "Somebody just ate my mother!"
For that way, of course, he could count on a quick trim
Without having to pay for the broken window.

THE MAN-AT-A-TABLE

There was a man-at-a-table
Who had himself a real bang-up time
Getting in and out of restaurants;
Only to have suddenly nervous strangers sit at him,
Often leaving fragments of their abandoned repasts . .
And once even a hurriedly detached hand,
That had been grinding out a cigarette.

THE TAME STREETCAR CONDUCTOR

There was a tame streetcar conductor
Who one day was considerably surprised
To have it suddenly bite his behind;
So next morning he reported for work
Disguised as a broad-minded chambermaid . .
And now lives with the company president's daughter.

THE WILY CARTOGRAPHER

There was a wily cartographer
Driving along with a load of melons
When he happened to notice some old ladies
Playing stickball beside the ruins of a greenhouse;
Rapidly unhitching, and swiftly standing
First on the right leg and then on the left,
He very quickly disappeared from sight.

THE CARELESS LITTLE SPY

There was a careless little spy
Who carried the Secret Code in the same briefcase
With the Master Plan and a wad of dancehall tickets;
Which may explain why some very Big Wheels
Are running about on their rims this morning.

THE FORGETFUL LITTLE
COMMUTER

There was a forgetful little commuter
Who one morning boarded a large sheepish dog
And rode to a splashing stop beside a fireplug;
Arrived home, he hung up his snapbrim wife,
And briefly kissing his hat, said, "Those damn forecasters!
I suppose that cloudburst is their idea of fair weather!"

THE LITTLE MAN WHO
SAW A GRASS

There was a little man who saw a grass
Kicking some beetles off the piano;
So he went to an old sage and demanded:
"Exactly whose chivalry does this defend?"
To which the old sage immediately responded:
"Quick! some water, bub — I smell beard-smoke!"

THE LOYAL STANLEY STEAMERITE

There was a loyal Stanley Steamerite
Who never got invited to parties;
So he let his mustache grow straight out
Until nobody whatever could get past him
Without first deeding over all their property.

THE OLD BRONCHOBUSTER

There was an old bronchobuster
Who read somewhere that the common chicken egg
Was descended from a tiny animal called "the spuze";
This thought so alarmed him that he ripped open
All his·old saddles and went around in snowshoes.

THE MAN WHO WAS
SHORTER THAN HIMSELF

There was a man two inches shorter than himself
Who always kept getting stuck in the sidewalk;
And when the curious townsmen came
To yank his arms and crush his hat,
He'd spit in the eye of the lean,
And steal the wallets off the fat.

THE CELERY-FLUTE PLAYER

There was a celery-flute player
Who got himself caught burning fire
On top of some old hoodlum's lake;
They wanted to hit him with a hammer,
But couldn't get up the admission
He would have charged them to see it.

THE GOGGLE-EYED
RABBIT-COUNTER

There was a goggle-eyed rabbit-counter
Who thought to divert himself by pretending to be
The statue-in-nude of the town's stuffiest old maid;
He did this so extremely well in fact
That she is now the father of three little marble generals.

PROMINENT COUPLE BELIEVED
PERMANENTLY STUCK TO PORCH

On impulse, to impress you, and remembering
How much in grade school you liked them,
It was I who had those thousand taffy apples
Delivered to your house —
After so many years!
Me, a humble but honest filing clerk,
And you, O little pig-tailed one, the Mayor's wife!
How was I to know you'd be off vacationing?
Anyhow, think how lucky you are . .
For I might have sent roses —
And then you'd of had big sharp-nosed bees
Lappin' at you instead of them contented bears!

ON THE PARKBENCH

On the parkbench sleeps a small bird-shaped man
In a tophat and orange-purple riding boots flecked
With chocolate, for he had spent the afternoon
In an ice cream saloon. Curled up in his lap
Is a very tall old lady; around them,
On the grass, behind the grass, and smack up
Against the grass, are suitcases, carafes, satchels,
Kegs, tubs, platters, sacks, jars . . and all filled
With the makings of exotic sandwiches. Ah . .
That's why the policeman looks so sallow —
He's a pot of mustard!

ON THE PARKBENCH

On the parkbench sleeps a tiger
With a very tall old lady
In his lap; she is so tall
(And so noisy) that her knees
Have attracted a pair of screechowls
To form on them a nest which sways.
This brings some rabbits, a blazilix,
A camel on a sled, seven frogs, a huge
Red mouse, a policeman, and an even
Taller old lady brandishing an electrified
Trumpet, to the scene; and to us
The timely remembrance of a dinner date.

AND WITH THE SORROWS
OF THIS JOYOUSNESS

O apple into ant and beard
Into barn, clock into cake and dust
Into dog, egg into elephant and fingers
Into fields, geese into gramophones and hills
Into houses, ice into isotopes and jugs
Into jaguars, kings into kindnesses and lanes
Into lattices, moons into meanwhiles and nears
Into nevers, orphans into otherwises and pegs
Into pillows, quarrels into quiets and races
Into rainbows, serpents into shores and thorns
Into thimbles, O unders into utmosts and vines
Into villages, webs into wholenesses and years
Into yieldings . . O zeals of these unspeaking
And forever unsayable zones!

AN "IMPRESSION GAZOOM"

I get a most definite "impression gazoom"
As I comb through my days as an opener
Of Kansas doors and shutter of Wyoming windows;
When you would come bustling out of the shack,
Your eyes like undone cakes grabbing me to pan,
Casting the tanner's abrupt needle into a bush,
Or behind the swing, for Wally Potts, barefoot
As usual, it being a time the brooks ranuvert
Like eager green pinkies along the town's thigh,
To find himself suddenly possessed of half
Laurinda Robert's bra, and standing, perchance,
Quite altogether through the other side
Of that old brick wall, where, was the night fine,
The woodcutters would park their long sleek yellow cars
And war their souped-up radios at one another.

LIKE I TOLD YOU

We headed out to the orchard
And looked a while
It seemed all right
The apples weren't complaining
The Bird of the Mountains
Was strolling around
Making up a little song
Maybe to the sun
Or for his special friends
Or his sweetheart
Or just to himself
And maybe for no reason
That anybody could tell you about
Sort of like I'm doing right now

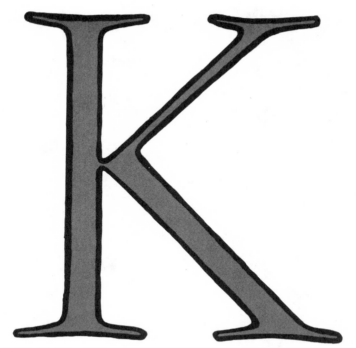

AFLAME AND AFUN OF WALKING FACES

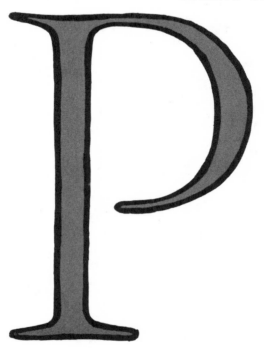

THE WALKING FACES

A tree grows beside a great road. Centuries pass, to be followed one day by two smiling children who lead a bright, spoon colored bird, upon whose twinkling and satiny foot vast congeries of faces are painted.

Perhaps the clowns again. Those other saints. Poor thinkama-jugs of an all too short eternity.

And so the children grow up, through their own sadness to another, and a far grayer, one. While feather upon bright feather spins earthward and dies. And always there is only the tree to remember, though itself forgotten in a flood of faces that hurriedly rushes nowhere.

Until that hour comes when the tree in its turn comes shattering down. . . wheels spinning like a pity of hands on an overturned schoolbus. Years and thrones gathered into the crowded nothing-ness.

— While, perhaps, the faces will not be seen again.

And now, if that be true, only the great road remains. Though, it would be wrong not to say, roads are limited in how they may be great.

HOW THE PROBLEM OF WHAT
TO HOLD CREAM IN
WAS EVENTUALLY SOLVED

Once upon a time a lovely little All-Blue-Pitcher fell sound asleep in the ram's-wool shop, and so was left the whole night there.

Hour on hour pludded by. And like fleece pouring out of a drum of snowy molasses the Moon edges ever nearer along the counter, along the soft down of the counter where she lay so fast asleep— his drake-cruel hands sluthening out slowly towards her... And from the Harbor of the Scolding Princesses comes the muffled murmur of a hacksaw as someone makes some last minute repairs on an old iron filing case such as were once used for storing away the illegible logs of long, forgotten sailing captains.

But now... the fliltering lips of the Moon slowly impress themselves upon her tiny flute-rilled ears. And a voice like dreamed fur whispers: "Oh wake, wake, my bonny one, my fair and bridey jewel... O less than the shadowy curving of thy cooft wee breasties are all the vain five-legged dog put on by Xerkrarrus now— and aye, by them begrifferdamnedandpigeonpuking legions of his, if it's a word of truth you're not afraid to meet this once in the world. Dust of the dust's dust and the white rain a-falling doon from the dead sky. . ."

Then, ah then does the little All-Blue-Pitcher awaken. . . While slowly creep the blind and cold snails of all the earth's hours into the milky wrinkling of that moment, to stay on there fast for an ever. . . Beauty gone in sorrow-joy to learn the strange gentleness of the Beast.

Temples like caked cream, beginning endlessly to crack wide open. White flies buzzing in the sun.

Even the lark, when in airiest song, must still have a bit of the trouble caught somewhere in his tune.

THE SCHOLAR: THE INSECT

The Graduate Graduate-Student walked precisely to and fro until he entered upon a rainy forest. Adjusting his peaked cap and frowning, he seated himself in the windish-swept place (a stumped clearing. . . broken beer bottles, the lesser part of a green rubber budat*). Shortly his wait was rewarded in the person of what he guessed to be a nude professor's wife, but which under intenter scrutiny he was able quite easily to mistake for an efficient and highly glossed canoe handle salesman. "I'm afraid not today," he declared himself with a wan grimace of camaraderie. "It just so happens that I have forgotten my pipe. Have you ever done that, I wonder? Fetching with you this curious object, instead...?" The Madilla Butterfly, and a fine handsome fellow was he; sassy, and all brightly ferrelled, certainly well over eight feet— considered most carefully, then said: "What gude top-toppa me sech a how she say pulla-chain-gurr-gurr dam same place tree-tree, huh, honay bon?" Following which, and profitting by a sudden, violent downpour, the Graduate Graduate-Student found himself in a position to yell up after his interrogator: "There is something to be said for that, I'm sure; and

*) A preventative for kyedorcity in cattle.

moreover, it's really I who am in your debt, sir, for the fact is, I don't, in any event, smoke."

Luckily for Vice, it is best known for the company it does not keep.

HOW WATER FIRST CAME TO BE TRACKED
ONTO BEDROOM FLOORS

One beautiful green evening the Clown Pippo, on the patched worsted point of sitting to his supper of stewed gull livers and turnip brains, plucked the opportunity to remark a magnificent Lion burning on the river which flowed past almost at his brightly tattered elbow.

"That," he was about to say, "is a horse of slightly nobler wing," when, in response to a comitious knock, down through the orange and whitish eye-rimmed alley a wall was swung back to admit a fair young choir singer, who was ever so nicely disguised in the skin of a cast-off zebra.

The excitement having licked off a bit — "How marvelously lucky for my neighbor, the flagitious parson," merrily laughed Pippo the Clown, as he gamboled on with a sad, withdrawn dignity to a still richer clump of feathery. "For truly, not every pyromane is considerate enough to supply his own best fireman."

Better a 1000$ bill with a slight tear in it than a plugged nickle with none atall atall.

204

THE HISTORIAN OF ORCHARDS

And said the wind: Sera nimis vita est crastina . . .
And said the waves: Star fra le due acque . . .
And said the weather: Burla burlando vase el lobo al asno . . .
And said the sky: Das Leben kann allerdings angesehen werden als
ein Traum . . .
And said an observer there: O beauté du diable! Tout passe, tout casse,
tout lasse . . .

Near what was once the boundary between Persia and a land then known as Ireland, under circumstances as remarkable as any truth, stood a beautiful little Cherry Tree.

One day a Snowflake, alighting on that branch nearest heaven, said: "There is, perhaps, another explanation, or, I might even say, another reason, for it."

"Oh—"

"You have spoken so quietly, so without the usual. . . pleading— I did not say pity, no, I could never bring myself to say that to you! But truly, if you will allow me plain speech in this place, this wondrous island realm, your words were lost, they did not reach me. I am more sorry than I can tell. . ."

"Oh my friend— and O my thousand thousand friend. — What was my world in all truth! Now with that other and another! O now on the wind. — See, there, they, too, in the darkening houses, must, at last, come to this. . ."

And said the Snowflake: "*Auch das Schöne muß sterben.* What else, oh what else has anyone ever found to say but that, dear little grandma. . ."

Is it not wonderfully strange that for the greatest journey so many have been content to slip into the nearest old coat of snow?

BEHIND THE CURTAIN,
THE CURTAINED BEHIND

Through some error Miss Agrilla Utus, a retiring old turtlologist's widow, swallowed off a quart of spiked rye whiskey. The first day drew to its close. But on the second a group of quiet young men fumed their way into the house. There ostensibly to check over the carpets and certain of the hall lamps, in reality they hoped to pilfer some of the choicer eggs for their own experiments.

While they were thus laying plans and finding inconspicuous nooks into which hats, gloves and topcoats might be left, a muffled voice suddenly addressed them from the top landing: "Ferncase? Is that you, Ferncase?"

The young men, taken at a total loss, could only finger over their college insignia and wait. Then one, doubtless made reckless by the overly fetid breath which poured down upon them, coughed, and again, this time even more loudly. . .

"Old Pal Old Pal Old Pal," resumed the voice, seeming, if anything, even more muffled now. "Oh Ferncase, dear, I knew, I knew you'd come! But hurry, please please hurry. . . I warned you you'd catch your death of cold going down into that frozen ground hunting more of those damn crawly things. But that can wait. That can wait. You hurry right on up here. . . There's a silly old woman hiding behind this curtain without a stitch on, and I can't get her to go to bed. Oh Ferncase, I can't I can't—"

There was the sound of helpless sobbing, followed by a tearing crash. Then silence.

After a moment one of the young men said, "Well. You know, I'd always heard it rumored that she took only the scantiest interest in his career. But now, *really.*"

If you would have your eggs sat on, it might be well to choose the smallest elephant you can find.

RIGHT NIECE, WRONG UNCLE —
OR VERSA VICE

A headlong Spinstress, who had only that sallow, unkempt morning returned after a lank absence to town, chanced to stumble on the Mayor in a huddle beside a rosy and plumpish wall; soupon, with perhaps less caution than sagacity, she at once sank her blushing teeth into his most exposed person.

Then it befell that the victim of this unseemly whim, descending to earth quite wreathed in frowns and ivy, beseeched purple heaven for some explanation of an action that was so grossly out of track with the high station at which he was in habit of getting off.

"Ah, you have come to the right one for an answer to that," cuttingly replied the Spinstress, while, with nearsighted vanity, she fingered her one concession to modern taste, a massive eyebrow through which a perfectly round pair of blue nostrils sniffed out at the world. "I had every reason to believe that you would not recall the particular incident in question. . ." And with the spidery gesture of one to whom even revenge must bring a web of mingled sweetness, she unlaced first one then the other of her furry yellow boottops and began hissingly to moisten the hem of her glistening blouse. "However, I am now doubly sure that you won't come dropping cigar ashes in my bathwater again, you three-faced old rogue you!" she added, as she gravely peered through the ragged, fat tear in the stone wall.

THE DOLT AND THE PRETTY DAMSELS

One brilliantly sunned afternoon a Dolt, whose literal-minded mother had kept a half inch eye on him ever since he was old enough to go see the man with the horse on his own, was agreeably astonished to discover a covey of Damsels bathing in a millpond above which hung a network of cleverly placed mirrors.

Now the Dolt had never seen anything like that before, and at first he thought they must be bags of some funny grain with wigs pasted on to hold their teeth in place. But as he drooled nearer he found them more and merrily unlike his mother, who had only that morning fallen through the bathroom transom of their new boarder, giving herself a broken leg and him a ticket for running through a red light while driving a stolen shower stall.

Ah then, alas, with such pretty unscolding cries, alas, alas and alas, they splashed out upon the bank, and all a-pink and a-golden-o — were blown as petals off across the drab cement of the field; were gone, gone, *gone!*

The poor Dolt, with all the fire turned out under his own particular little phoenix, could only softly glubber: "I wonder where they got such fine round little peaked hats of moonfur to squeeze in upon their chests like that. *Gosh...* a person would need hands as nice smelling as false teeth paste before you could touch one of them, I bet."

WHAT'S SAUCE FOR THE TOMATO

On one of the grubbiest days ever seen anywhere an underheeled youth named Wendell Skurppy was slupping along a grayish weakfishlane in a certain dasmell clump of stloumo brickbushes, when he suddenly rung into a plump foreheaded, buck-tousled Sassiety Belle. Pleased no lard by her frostily expensive frigidaire manner then by the cadillacical way she carried herself, he was at flust cluck dumb, but sloob ladaged callowly to swike up the thousand haller-*Bill!* which had fallen so cloyly from one of her biliousing adorsal shoulder blubs.

Within a few monuments they were swoon grooving hoppily together along a nearthigh fignewtonpk, breathing deeply of the acrid odor rising from statues of past greats (now carefully guarded over by three legged wolfhounds), and nubbling juicily at the tiny brown oranges which the peeling old S. B. took from time to time and a drawer in the highboy-like neck of her more than half gilded chauffeur.

"I suppose you were born all luscious and fresh and nearly naked right here in town?" she asked, her tongue slipping in a most freudening fashion.

"Oh no, I came here as a small, jewel-covered elephant," he

replied, showing her a slip of his own; though quakely he added, "I mean, as a small boy."

"Hmmm!" she remarked; adding, "Shake it up a little there, Gliskens. Some of us have work to do, even if you haven't. Put it into second now and drive on up to my chateau 'long side good old Oyster Bed Cove." And, beginning a rather roguish and one sided pillow fight with the now far from merely underheeled Wendell Skurppy, she assured him huskily, "And as for you, I'm going to see to it that you at least *leave* this town a man. . ."

Whereupon, gleaming into the rear-view mirror, the chauffeur Gliskens said, "It'll be many a golden moon again before there's an unfairer exchange than that."

NO TITLE ON THIS'N
SMO KEY JES KEP AE ATIN
M OFF FARTAS DYNEMIT PIE

Tired of having the ne'er-do-well sons of the town's better classes sneak in to gobble up his paste every time his back was turned, a clever young paperhanger at last hit on the stratagem of staking out a dragon within easy compass of the pot. All went very smoothly indeed until one day Young Smoky got hungry— and not just ordinary dragon-hungry, but hungry for those tender little calves slippers which only grow in distant swamps and behind women's gyms. Since to tackle the swamp beds would occasion a trek of upwards of eighty miles, roughly, even by fast plane, the resourceful paperhanger (whose name was Puddie F. Gilette) eagerly threw himself into the campaign for building funds. Benefits, bazaars, entertainments where fat officials raced to thrilling ties with gauntly competitive tigers. . . And before many moons had passed, there, under the gayly burnished walls of flawless glass, modest little calves slippers began timidly to flex and unflex their jellyish, brown toes. Never had Young Smoky had it so good— he ate and ate until he became like a candle burning happily away at both ends.

And today, a proud sign in imitation brass hangs over the

hose and slip case just as you go into the locker room; distracting our eyes for a moment, we may read:

P. Fustus Gilette, Superintendent of Hand etc. Towels, Soaps, Foot etc. Powders, as well as of Various Other Random etc. Concessions.

He who flees the pastepots surely has scant right to complain at being slopped up by those of a rather more fleshly kind.

OR as Confusions keep
on a tellin' us'
Lesson less about
MOURN & MOURN

THE TALE OF ROSIEBOTHAM

A very lovely Rosiebotham was strolling early one summer's evening through an akrono when, in a place where many square uglinesses grew side by side, a Mrdannytuttle rudely struck her acquaintance with a glossy bow.

"Would you guess," says he, "that I've a fleck of something on my heart that has a most pretty leg growing right down out of it?"

And shyly she answers, "Oh sir, if looks like yours were only obstetricians, what a fine family I'd have. But alas, I am simply in process of taking a pleasure walk, roomkey held tight in my hand— for otherwise, you see, there is a nasty landlord to be considered."

"Him, Miss?"

"Yes, indeed, indeed! A man of incestuous temperament!"

The Mrdannytuttle patiently waited until an ambulance had splashed to a halt between two crowded trolleys, then he laughed and declared, "Danger, yes, yes, I could see that if he were anyone else. But really now— your own father!?"

"I never *quite* thought of it in that way," she admitted, and followed him into a gaudy emporium where they together enjoyed three frosted grape frappés.

Now when they were outside again, the Rosiebotham remarked impetuously, "And would you know, he's even got one of those light-up neckties. The fiend!"

"Ah-*huh*, tell me— What does his say?" eagerly asked the Mrdannytuttle.

She hesitated, blushed, and tremblingly told him: "'How's about a kiss, Kiddo?'"

Then quickly the Mrdannytuttle led her into a darkened alley. "Have yourself a gander at mine," he said huskily.

And, after a moment— "Oh— I'm *terribly* sorry— But I couldn't possibly be your Valentine," she said.

THE OEILLADER WITH AN INDOLENT, GREASE-SMEARED MUSTACHE

A Hanger-On who had never really succeeded in coming to grips with himself, chanced one evening to notice a streetcar on the ledge just outside his window.

Thinking it a scaffolding of some kind, he leaned forward on his careless cigaretteflowered couch and asked the motorman: "Am I right in my surmise that you are planning to do a bit of scrubbing? I take it that that *is* a red floormop in your hand?"

Across the street, and below them, the blurred figure of a man beating five drums lounged in a doorway.

"I couldn't tell you, Rosebud," the motorman answered, beginning to edge off one of the broken steps. "You'll have to ask the conductor's wife. She's the one had it on her head when the track buckled, not me."

It's a strong wind that doesn't blow some fellow with a bang against some unsuspecting house or other.

AN ADVENTURE WITH JUBILOSO GIOCHEVOLE

Dans un bal les bateaux sont le sexe timide et le sexe décent . . .

Once upon a time a fat little boat named Jubiloso Gioche-
vole chanced to find himself on the floor of a great and splendid
banquet hall, where a nobly impressive dance was in progress.
At once the cynosure of all those jeweled eyes and quite without
training for his new role, he was more than pleasantly comforted
by the behavior of two ancient and resplendent ladies, who,
sensing a rare merit and holiness in his demeanor, without pre-
tense or ostentation straightway shed themselves of their sequined
and shiningly expensive gowns of coxcomb satin and vaulted—
with thunder of rings and swash of unstringing pearl necklaces
— into his waiting stern.

Across the fogfurred river, in the Bandstand of the Lopsided
Crowns, the assinine braying of a long eared ballteam could be
heard; while in the nearerby General Solamabangdi Cemetery
came the mournful khakiing call of some poor, very dead bird.

And down the plateau, in a red flanneled tide from one
clothesline to the next poured a strain of old men clutching
gleeful buttonsnippers; as meanwhile through all the famous
manors borne on the winds of as many young crowing rudesters,
funbuffeted maids made the welcome rosy with their golden

218

scullering. — Ah yes, ah yes! It's not every day that oil is struck in the King!

And who else but our dear friend Jubiloso Giochevole, finding the river suddenly almost deserted, would be the last to be let in on news of that kind. . .?

Though, as it worked out, he had a great deal of fun anyway — or so he wrote to one of his older brothers, who, having been junked only a short time before, was only now beginning to appreciate what it means to languish in the China trade.

OIL'S WELL

THE WOLF THAT CRIED OHBOY OHBOY

At the very foot of the worn path a fuster of straggling st.john'swort treaded gingerlessly under the cobblenailed sky. But along the main street itself all the storeawnings were down, and out from under their purple and brown wrinkles, very like those a worried old skinless giraffe might have, a tall little man peers drunkenly, the left shoe of one of his stilts caught in a grate. And far from idle himself, Oatis Oggle had just finished transferring the soundest of his furniture and other effects to an expensive mansion which overlooked the town, to mention only one instance of its churlish attitude. Hence he had every excuse to settle back and enjoy the chagrin of his much too-cocky wife. More, in fact, than opportunity, for he had quite reckoned without the Bailey Sisken Basses who, somewhat exercised by the sudden intrusion of the leather-aproned and -lunged movers in the still hours of the night, burst hotly from the rooms of their butler and maid respectively, causing poor Oggle almost to reconsider the wisdom of his impulsive manoeuver. For, as the old saying would have it, often what is done with rash intent may as surely reap dissent.

But in this event, Oatis Oggle, after suing the Bailey Sisken

Basses for lack of moral torportude, was not only enabled to return with a considerate fortune to his own spouse, but even more easily persuaded to squander the interest alone on a truly fetching young lady who brought him nothing save unremitting happiness and ill-concealed satisfaction.

Alas, Lust, even more than Greed, is what makes racehorses.

PERPETUAL EMOTION OR HOW-COME A GATOR IN THE LOBBY?

A traveling Contortionist & a Clergyist's shy sister'n law were comforced by don't of no rooms be ye dad'r dame a New England type night to spend in such a blizzard never seen in Hell even! In that period every decent hotel strictly observed the ordinance behooving Bundling—it wasn't the cold give them blue noses. Wicked flesh be sure they'd heard of. Hence the serpent-like Beast near the sign-in desk—ask that pair a bove! Odd buffer...& him ticklish to boot!

SURE CURE FOR A COLD

In an ugly tan pisgahwva there once lived a Rhodacary. A long low whistle from being ugly, on any hand she looked all made of little birds, which someone had sewed together with very special care.

Now one day a big yellowmustached Frankxgillett, who was every bit as keen as a bucket of frozen gravel, happened to sit down on her in the plumbing fixtures works where she modeled furniture for 'those ladies who demand that ethereal touch,' as the ads proudly phrased it. He later explained that he was under the impression somebody musta left their bearskin on the seat; for, among much else, he was also addicted to footballing.

So, scarcely more than a few weeks had passed when, rather than suffer his snuffling proposals at any greater length, the Rhodacary's mother, herself an accomplished eavesdripper, proceeded to give her talented daughter's consent to the unhappy union. For that is exactly what it turned out to be.

On the very afternoon of the wedding itself the groom, doubtless thinking to show off his great wealth, rammed a thick stack of fifty dollar bills down the throat of the wrong horse. To be sure, not every young bride is fortunate enough to see her new

husband buried with a good luck sign planted square in the middle of his forehead. The horse, whose professional name was Loonbait Louie, was ordered stuffed, after first being given one shot for the money.

And our no longer poor but even lovelier Rhodacary, her own mistress at last, went rapidly to pieces— first to one which jutted up out of the top of a great dreary rock called nyny, from whence, amid the shrill cawing of yellow cabs and the gilty sobbing of many another wee wren forced to glow in plush pens lined by whole and leering hawgs, she sent many touching and thoughtful gifts to her dear dear mother. Among them, an almost new pennant with Yarvard on one side and Hale on the other, for, while she wanted to send her mother off on the right cultural foot, so to speak, she also dearly wanted to do all she reasonably could to avoid those stupid factional fights which so often spring up in homes reserved for indigent old ladies.

THE THREE VISITORS

An insouciant little Pelagic Breeze, finding himself in somewhat elegiacal surroundings with the declension of night, stealthway penetrated into the shanty of a certain unjocund Cup-fashioner, where, dismayed by the powdery glabrosity of his host, he began, ebulliently, to cozen some exiticial catholicon.

Soft on the heels of a prelusive moment, Nookie Belle, the arcadian mistress of an old codger gone only recently hibernal, tapped ever so tridently on the circus posters which hung in pragmatic abandon under the stained lintel. "Are you there, Mr. Tessis?" softly, softly she called.

"Why, yes, of course, where else?" the dry-cheeked little Pelagic Breeze replied with stridulous haste, emboldened out of all countenance.

"Ah, then, I'm not too late! That is good, good, very good indeed; for, you see, dear Mr. Tessis, I've fetched you a quantity of real clay, clay of the earth, earthy kind. . . So now, oh now, my dear Mr. Tessis, you won't have to go on hacking bits out of your own flesh, so to speak. . ."

But our little Pelagic Breeze was already well into his third ocean before the young goddess, who was as beautiful as she was kind, got anywhere near to catching on to the lie.

If perfection could be practiced by everybody, what a very, very mournful noise would assail those soft white ears up there!

MOONDOGG AND THE ONE-ARMED DENTIST'S SISTER

Under silver maskery of hours like frozen waves— when those whom eternity accosts have palely come— within sound of the chimney's gray-petalled wound, Moondogg quietly waits, waits for the maiden of gray tears to climb to a place beside him.

Blurred golden eyes peer up from the winding motorway, while furry lids softer than a bat's nipples open and close over harbor and listening vineyards, silhouettes against which the grieving hands of fogbells vainly beat. . . peril and longing bedded down like sad crones in a stuff any child might pick apart as easily as that hangman of romance the cottony breath of a thief falsely accused (perhaps of one's very own family). . .

Now, in the only moment for that, she climbs, like a struggle

of scissors, to where the sky ends so unimportantly in a roof—
the sky which is an animal will ride or rest on almost anything,
trains, used grapeskins, heads of sick old whores, slopping up
and down in crummy roominghouses ready, at the droop of a
rat, to go off on the gaffing route if they so much as get an un-
cancelled postcard from some daughter or other who thinks she's
too good to watch a hairy blue duck making a batch of fudge
unless she has her pink, formal gloves on—; thereupon Moon-
dogg inquired, "Well— that is, tell me first, did you have a
nice day?" and he falls to kissing her dangling arms and forehead.

Birds of ice with blunted gray beaks tear at the shrouding
waves. O then sobbing into his cruel pale curls, she will answer:
"Take me with you! O now take me, take me with you. . . In
three weeks less a day I shall be fiftyseven years old.

"O the songs and tales you have given me of your world. —
Soon, soon whatever might have been for me. . . look! the cold
long dark, and I have had no life I have never lived at all. . ."
She continued on in this vein for some little while.

Moondogg let her chatter herself quite out, then, grinning he
uncoiled one protracted statement after the other, each seem-
ing to have more flurry about nothing than the other. . .
". . . and so my father made an absolute, a preposterously final

sort of fool of himself; I know I, for one, excusing the expression, would never have thought it feasible to have, say, well—, *pink* lilies growing up out of horsemanure— would you? truly now, would you? Of course not! It's positively vulgar, if not disgusting. . . Scarce wonder they locked him out."

"Take me away! O take me away with you!"

Hungrily in and out run his white tongues, and Moondogg says with kindness strange (and roll waves of pitiless wonder! the faces shaped in ice and the fire born of the watching darkness): "Cling you fast in upon my belly. Hold there. Hold— In the color of tears is the speech of mankind made; in that of skulls the bravest squeak from any bright old lad. . . Watch it now! I may prove a bit. . . ticklish."

"Oh, there's one other thing," she pants up through his stiff, cold fur. "Please fly me through that damn brother of mine's office just once more before we set off. Oh boy. . . Oh boy. . .! (I left the windows all open.) Oh, boy! Wait'll that prissy bum gets a load of *us!*"

Fortunately there still are ways of teaching dentists not to shove their arms halfway down the throats of nervous patients.

GAUNT EVE IN THE MORNIN'

It was one of those days that seem to make their way in without anybody noticing much about it. Mrs. Arglutt folded her sweaters and waited.

Pretty soon Juggie the Boddy-Fann arched his short though lithe body over the curb. Oh, yes, Mrs. Arglutt thought. There's you all right— and next it'll be that sleazy gilled postman! Oh, yes, and him all as shy as a beat-up lark on last summer's hammock. And suddenly her musing took an audible direction: "I wonder. Oh, yes, I do at that. I just got me a hunch that it do a bit of whistlin', too. *Him— him* and those pretentious sleeve bands and gold bead moccasins of his!"

And there he was. It was exactly ten of eight, not one iota different from any other day! There he was peering in through the window on the sunporch, his glinty ox's eyes fixed on her person. — "I just know I must look like a big pink sponge. . . Oh, what a habit to get into!" Mrs. Arglutt said, pretending to address a stack of those old fashioned postcards which specialize in winter scenes and reary skirted bathers on long closed beaches. One after the other she lifted her woolen, salmon colored sweaters from their adjoining stack and pressed them over her swirling chest. Behind her a pane in the reinforced window tinkled out— Oh, damn! Mrs. Arglutt thought, her blush deepening perceptibly, whether from exasperation or the sudden snuffling at her shoulder blades, it would be hard to say. "That's the fourth this week already," she mumbled with a little shiver of nervous excitement.

And then at last the clock was clanging the hour. — *Now* she could breathe again, he was gone. Like that-poof!

When she felt her strength returned enough she sighed into her corset, meanwhile waddling first forward then back in the imitation hip dance she'd picked up at one of her perennial Saturday movies— and it was not until she had shrugged her slip and torn kimono-style housecoat down over her frizzy, graying hair that she permitted herself a half-petulant, half-gleeful speculation: Oh, yes, oh yes indeed! First it was that great silly, mustard-flecked mustache of yours, then it was those two geranium-pot-red shredded wheats you stuck on yourself for eyebrows— Oh, yes, you sure handed me a laugh with those correspondence school disguises of yours, dearie! And, next— Ah, but why should I look ahead to spoil your fun! You poor silly... who could miss knowing that big foot-long nose of yours? Let alone all bandaged out like a basket of diapers.

And suddenly Mrs. Arglutt sank down on an old sofa whose torn cover was littered with movie and confession magazines— and lowering her swollen gray face into her fat, braceletted arms, she began, helplessly, to cry. And Mrs. Arglutt thought: Ah, yes, there'll come the mornin' when you swallow that precious government whistle of yours altogether. . . And oh then it'll be that I have to watch the split ends of its string disappearing like the sad whiskers of some modern snake down to investigate the congestion of still another poor apple.

THE UNCLAIMED BEAVER

One foul day an Inamcshoon was squatting beside a wishbone vine thinking 'Better a rich young man's playtoy than something a poor old duffer would come round all the time dropping his cheap gray cigar ashes and hair on,' when a big Chuckbailey, its gold tooth slicked back from receding lips, presented and gave voice: "With you over there, Honay, and me cossing away yonder here, no wonder our youngins have had to wait so long for their own proper and fittin' parents. . ."

Then the Inamcshoon cried in a doubt: "Oh sweet bits! If only that candle of yours had a light on it, a bad half the women in town would be well singed."

High above them, in a shiny bald cypress, a twain of little scarlet bushtits were acrobirding happily, their gray chests and greener feet contrasting in brilliance with the heavy, dullish fragrance of the needles and the darkness, which had just pitched down. Like a bear begging the arm of some reluctant hunter, the Chuckbailey fetched its hand out and called again: "Then they finally did get round to planting your old man, huh?"

"Well, y-es, that was all right, after he had turned down every drink of good corn we kep' a-offerin' him— hell, it went on like that for purty nears better'n two weeks. He was always stubborn, Pa was, but not *that* stubborn. But now you take the old 'oman— all us kids got to callin' her that from Pa, I reckon — now *she'd* shove you real close on some dang pipped-up thinkin', she would. Well, now, sir, when she went 'long to the buryin'. — Stop your doin' thet! Oh that poor old 'oman, jest like a bitty little bald baby, 'septin' she had kinda spotted gray hair that grows right down past her chest— There we was, as I said, all a-standin 'blowin' our nose and things, when Jed he looks round. 'Now where'd thet old 'oman go!' Jed he says, —all jumpy like.

"Poor little ragged greasy thing. . . You know how curious she allus used to be aboutin' holes—"

"S'ppose you mean that old 'oman Ma of yours?" put in the big Chuckbailey.

"'Member that old long fur hat she'd wear most like a piece of cardboard you'd plaster up a window with— Why, hell, she even wore it on her head to the attic. That's where she did her sleepin'."

"This is that old 'oman Ma of yours, you're a-fixin' to tell me about?"

"Wull naow—" went on the yaller haired Inamcshoon. "Thet

old long fur hat hain't on hits nail 'bove the woodshed dooar. And I *jest know* she'd be a-comin' lookin' for it onless. . . onless'n somethin' was a-holdin' her down— Like, say, mebby a little ole hole in the groun'. . ."

"Thet's a mighty good way of doin' things. I once't had an old grandpap allus uster 'clare: 'Boay, Ah figgers hit a-this'n way— Dirt is jist erbout the oney meat nobody kin complain of not gittin' enough of.' So-o— Let's you and me fry us up a little chicken, huh?"

HE DIDN'T KNOW THE SON WAS LOADED

An Edodell, one quite late and starless night, believing that the window belonged to a certain Maziefeccio, climbed instead into the one of a Mrspjjones, with the resulting dislodgement of several pots, among them one for flowers and two for a somewhat more fugitive usage.

"Whatever are they yelling about down there, Herbert?" a sleepy voice greeted him from the darkness.

"Beg pudon, I think you've made a mistake, too," the Edodell simply replied. He was under average tall, salloweyed, given to stealing furtive glances at the legs of horses on circus posters.

"Eeh— So I have. Oh, *here's* the lightcord. Damn, for a minute there I thought somebody was pulling at the pigtail of my wig. But, you see, I have made a mistake. Just between us, *my* Herbert would never dream of going to call on a strange lady with a wet pantsfront showing. Besides—" and she chuckled, revealing a set of uneven gums— "the funny thing is, Herbert has been dead for well on to twenty-three years now. He was what they used to call a trainchaser. Poor dear. You see, he finally *did* catch one, a great big shiny rootsnorter of a one, but wouldn't you just know, the damned thing was going the wrong way. But here I am jawin' away while I'll bet you're hungry enough to eat a mess of Arizona sardines without even botherin' to open the can. You'll find some in the drawer of the bureau that big galvanized pot I used to keep geraniums in rolled under."

At a lack of anything more exciting to do, the Edodell spent two long thumbnails accepting her kind invitation, dripping self-consciously from one foot to the other as he did so. When hi! lo! out of the bureau drawer sprang a little guy who, brandishing an old-fashioned horsepistol, cried: "No ornery galoot is agonta hold up this here stage coach while old Houston Herbie Junior's on deck!"

Then, after an abrupt, soiled herringbone twinkling, the Mrspjjones said proudly, "That was sure a smart move changin' them house numbers. Reckon that must be about the twelfth-thirteenth tonight already."

"Shull's I close what's left of the winder now, Maw?"

"Shore you kin, Son. The sooner you git that new one up, and the pots all back in their place, the better it'll be. But fust, throw his pants down onto the runnin' board of that crockery cart he fell into— Mmm... two sawbucks and a trey of fins in his hippocket. This rate, we soon kin go off a-lookin' round for your Paw down the shaft of thet goldmine somewheres in good ole Nevady City. Twenty-odd years is a long time, Son, — and with thet good sharp haid of your Paw's, who knows what he may've struck by now."

TAT FOR TWO

When Harry and Edgar were little boys in very gay ratatan shortsuits their mothers were in habit of taking them, either on tedious hikes, that were oftentimes depressing and tiring as well, or to see the former's Aunt Nettie, a formidable and notoriously predatory woman.

However, this frequently turned out rather better than any of them had any real right to expect, for not only are things someways offpoint in sober prospect, they are even more occasionally no less keenly absurd from the vantage furnished by memory. Certainly even the most quiescently supercilious of individuals would have been forced, and that, readily, to the admission of some considerable hesitation in regard to the moral advisability of taking such mere pips of circumstance to visit "*that* woman."

In the very first place, to begin only there, there was the temptation— and what a very real one it was!— instinct in an unshaved leg. . . More might be said— much, much more . . . However—!

Is it worth saying that little Harry and Edgar lost a moment in succumbing to an opportunity of such attraction (and menace) to their as yet nascent talents? We think it is, and for a reason no more complex or convoluted than this: Our little sillies, despite all the bravery of their tanned salmon colored, wedge shaped caps and equally aggressive nonchalance, had promptly and joyously leapt upon that very particular moment as being the most convenient envelope for the enclosure of a bit of sprightly goldfish-strawing— the one useable momento of their increasingly irksome hiking expeditions.

Oh well may you ask: What is worse than a bad woman? And oh well may we answer: Why, man— What else but a good one cut in two. . .

BOTTOMS UP

Now once there was a Roydabbit who, to offset a strong tendency to the puny, had at last weakly given way to the temptation of fancying himself a weightlifter, now (fortunately) unemployed.

He lived in a small hollow nokomisill with a ribcovered Berthamae and an old hairbrimmed grumpus named Maknowsbest, both of whom claimed to have his number, the one that comes just before one.

It chanced that one very buickiful morning, as dark sandhued vines of claustrodioxide were weaving round the huge happy green poster which acted as steeple on the almytbuckian chapel, the Roydabbit was just in point of emerging from a drugstore with a set of fencing foils, two boxes of greenish banana shaped generators and half a dozen coils of highly magnetized wire, when he happened to fall in with his loudly gesticulating mate and female parent. The former, luckily, was protected by hipboots and a rubber bee hunter's mask and cape. But Maknowsbest— ah, she proved herself to be a tale with a somewhat different end.

It had befallen that some years before she had been hit in

the head by a wedge while out stretching her legs on a motor trip one day through the north woods. However, with little more than the loss of a clump of rather badly worn hair, some visiting firemen did succeed in breaking her sudden and irresistible attraction for the exercising wire. Indeed, they brought her to with such extremely diligent care that Maknowsbest spent the next few days leading them in window busting forays on all the neighboring towns around, and wasn't ever quite sober again until she passed on through a window in a signboard eight stories above the scatteringly crowded main street.

But poor Roydabbit— ah, he was surrounded immediately by a glad crying group of Katinkajoneses, their distinctive markings clearly revealed under their coats of volley ball and beach umbrellaing: "Oh do show us that handpress again!" "*And* those fascinating pushups!" "When does our turn come to stand on your shoulders?" And so saying each grasped a foil and was sent shooting upward to the magnetized wire. —

"Oh!" "Oh!" "Oh!" "Oh!" — And oh how the Roydabbit's thin knees did bulge down over his shoetops, just with the strain of holding that spinning catherine wheel up out of reach of a throng of salesmen in a definite buying mood.

And oh how they spun and spun and spun... those swirling

fleshpink lilies — "Oh!" "Oh!" "Oh!" "Oh!" — A dazzling raiment indeed... while like a rain of petals down from the jackknifing necks of so many swans, a scatter of middy blouses and gay black silk shorts and badminton sandals... falling, falling on the bemussed crowd... And yet, oddly enough, the voice of the Berthamae contained an unmistakable note of severity in it as she declared: "So! You bent-leg bum you— Now I know why you come home at all hours with footprints smeared all over your nice clean shirts!"

And with a vestige of grim hauteur she broke one of the banana shaped generators from its box, — She sighted carefully up at the pinkly twirling petals. — And she let fly. —

"Oh!" "Oh!" "Oh!" "Oh!" — "Ooooh!"

CHICKEN FRIED IN HONEY

Clarence Snull, who had come to suspect that heaven needed more than one penny candle for proper lighting, found himself by easy degrees with the yearn to marry nicely and to live, if not happily, then at least with all his appetites, be they corporal or even of a less spiritual sort, something more than just well taken care of. For his part, let it be said now, he wanted something other than people customarily put in their hair; so far was this true, that it was the local Croesus, a Teddia Henatoe, who had unconsciously managed to insinuate herself in his.

Now the late Baron Wartley had been a noisy, foulmouthed oaf, with considerably more than an ordinary penchantius as a cut-up; and perhaps never more so than on the occasion of his being clawed to death by a nesting ibis which he had locked away in the cellar with one of his poorer nephews. Although this happened a good twenty years ago, that small boy is not only still bald but the most careful and extreme caution must be exercised in choosing maids of a peculiar type whose only duty is to sit very quietly on his head at night.

But however haunted in life she was by her husband's grammatical nastities, even Teddia will be the first to admit that the

Baron does lay most goldenly indeed now. You will remember that it was he who patented The Spokey Hula Queen, a phone-booth not to be confused with the Inquisition's much gentler "Iron Maiden"; and to his credit, too, must go that innocent-appearing seat cushion which has proved so useful in throwing strangers together at church socials — we refer, of course, to the famous Wartley Simulated-Elephant Windbreaker.

So one spring morning Clarence went bouncing off in hopes of receiving a good account for himself. "I just only hope she's not down in the garden pavilion with Torgas as usual," he told himself with the tone of one snuffling dead cigar ash through a borrowed straw. Now and then a small boy passed whistling shrilly, a long grimacing line of cows trailing behind him, tails held stiffly aloft under a brilliant gaiety of balloons. On the edge of a brown field and a barnroof an old woman with an eggcrate clutched under either arm was staring reproachfully up at a rusted tin weathercock, whose days of usefulness even in his special province were long since down the drain. From time to time she smote the tobacco colored gingham at her knee and spat disgustedly into the creaking wind.

Noticing on a sudden a fence of barbed rails Snull thoughtfully slapped his election buttoned beret upon first one raised sneaker then the other and declared: "I bet Torgas only rented that flashy admiral's suit of his. Besides, I'll fire the rat!— I mean, besides, I don't consider him to be a very good butler, anyway." With which happy decision behind him, he was able, after several false starts, to succeed almost in clearing by the crotchfirst method the dungaree-pennanted fence. A painfully short while after this experience he encountered the widow of his dreams emerging from a bamboo pavilion, the butler Torgas close as a mustard plaster at her elbow. From head to foot both were dressed entirely in feathers.

"Well, well. . ." Clarence declared, in a masterful effort to show himself equal to any emergency.

"Chicken pickin'," the butler Torgas remarked with a nonchalance that nearly smacked of the laconic, as he began rapidly to fashion a row of impromtu epaulettes across his downy, wire-haired chest.

"Oh Mr. Snull!" cried Teddia Wartley-Henatoe all in a flustery splutter. "It seems that Gassie and I have just had the most darling experience, but not only that, my dear Mr. Snull— Oh could you ever guess, I wonder! we've had an even more darling omen, as well! Do you remember— but of course you don't! But, *anyhow*, there used to be all along the ceiling a whole shelf of enormous crocks simply cram full of honey. Well!" And laughing happily she threw herself under Torgas the butler's protective wing— "They're not there now, Mr. Snully-Wully... *And* we're planning to fly right off and get married!"

After they had gone, Clarence walked glumly into the pavilion and throwing himself on the torn-up mattress, burst into laughter and tears; for his sweat shirt was ripped in several places.

HOW OSTRICHES CAME TO HAVE THROATS
LONG ENOUGH TO GET GOLF BALLS STUCK
IN THE MIDDLE OF

Her tail tied in a slipknot to a pink ogeechee lime tree by a mischievous young Ostrich, the Fearsame Queen of the Jungle regarded dourly the thrashed, flat tundra, brooding perhaps of some hard way of returning the compliment. So, most sweetly at last she called: "Oh Audry, honey chile, I am so ferociously pleased that you have honored me with your ingenious prank." Whereupon brightly the little Ostrich shuffled gulpingly forward off the links, his demeanor an open scorn of the whole race of caddies, who, it would certainly seem spend most of their time dashing madly about with the seats gone out of their pants. "How come, Queenie kid?" he bawled in a most jerky and disconcerting fashion. "Just put your head in here, dearie," the other roared gently, with a drooling nod at his footiwork. "And when I pull, you back up and see if you can kick that stupid boy with the nettle briars stuck all over his rear elbow."

Better to be threatened with a bad rule than measured with a good rope.

A CASE OF UNMISTAKABLE IDENTITY

The Great Detective was called to a small, worried town to investigate a report of blue people. "To begin with," he told the constable in charge, who was vainly trying to unlock his hand-cuffed wrists with a buttonhook borrowed from an old hip-yellow-shoed temperance worker whom many a drunk had taken a shine to, "I smell that you've been drinking. And at a horse trough— that much I don't need my long, bent microspipe for: unless, bore this in mind, that's just your own personal way of trying to disguise yourself as a skunk of loose habits."

Glancing idly through the cobwebs which served for windows, he watched two lovers carrying eager, naked blankets thread their way through the crowd, which consisted of a small man in a lavender beret who was stealing occasional glances at an unde-veloped roll of film. Then, noticing that several savage cows were about to catch the eight o'clock train just short of the station, he thought quite enough time had been wasted on this particular case, and proceeded to solve it without further delay: "I hap-pened to notice," he said, "a nudist colony just as the train almost tips over from a sudden weight-shift up along the cliff there. And I know, too, that you boys have been doing an uncommon

amount of fingerprint-taking lately— So, quite naturally, since there is no way of knowing where their sleevecuffs end, you've just been forced to do what I'd call a good, all-over job of it."

Hence it is that man is the only oyster with a head of hair that people are always putting and taking woolen drawers on and off of.

NOT ALL TOWELS COME FROM TURKEY

Innate modesty and poverty are, at best, little governable under even the most propitious circumstances; but, with a doting mother round his neck, and the sympathy of his elders scarcely more than a vague, withdrawn belching over feasts rather less palpable than unseen, Gus B. Marblecake finally applied for and was got to the position of head dryer in Mrs. Suddsineri's, an establishment where women only old might tea and soak in the past and far hotter steam.

There, soapfooting about from one grayly streaming stool to the next (in need of a touch of mansage): or: (perhaps just for a friendly jab up under the badly torn robe that had to be bought fresh each morning), poor Gus had his work clucked out for him keeping 'the balls a-bearing' — a phrase much favored by Ma Goatbane, whose idea of hirsute decorum demanded a sight more from him than the customary mustache-trimming.

But what irritated him to the point of diving suddenly over benches into open lye vats, when all the doors of the reducing cabinets happened to be rudely closed to him, was to have his mother grate round like an old disheveled possum pup, her long toenails squirking into his adams apple while she'd say something perhaps like: "Whyinel don't you go out and come back with a nice big bottle of ice cold beer? Or at least a shave! You couldn't have been listening very good!— I'm your mother, and pretty damned tired acting like a little bare two-faced Moses up in these here bushes!"

An ass loaded down with the burden of another is never more doubly so.

EVEN THE KRAKEN MUST HAVE HIS SPIEL

There was once a gently made Kraken under whose frontal neck squirmed a row of spindling green legs which culminated in badly worn carpet slippers, and these, in the main, of dubious fit. Now this did not for long escape the envious notice of his grumpy comrades; so, after a few short centuries, they gave him pain to realize that his continued presence was regarded as being not only strictly undesirable to them but positively anathematical to every cherished ideal of krakendom.

So — go he must; and that, unslowly. The night was cold ... even colder on land; close above tenebrous star huddles twitched grimly. Our poor, bewildered friend came ... at dripping last... to a house, a very big one, impressive with two front doors, and even supplied with an auxiliary cellar just under the driveway. Here, thank god!! lights were lit! and on a high balcony a thousand Persian horns were being softly agitated. At any rate, it was s-o-m-e-t-h-i-n-g!

Propelling his ice-corroded muzzles against a sweeping fret of windowpanes, to his glad delight he was instantly overjoyed to behold a wonderfully splendid table before which lolled a good five and seventy wee sapid orphans, a profusion of crumbs and buttons fatly popping off their greasy-snug suits.

Is it any wonder that, with some impatience, he beckoned to a lovely suede-faced lady in a low-cut shawl of peeling gold mesh whose legs were bowed nearly as double as her chin under frosty trays of sugar cookies and champagne buckets? but ah, how slowly, even so, did she roll to the massive, harpists'-picks-studded gate... *there!* at last she is throwing back the first bolt, and now another, another another, until all twenty three have been thrown! — "Good-evening, Mrs. Herbcrest," she greeted him warmly. "I scarcely recognized you without the glasses you borrowed from me early last summer. Land's sake, I do hope you haven't broken them... I've been eating any number of silly things, bits of teacups, part of that greedy little Thompson girl's finger... why, only day before yesterday I toasted up a whole set of my very prettiest napkins. How amused the children were to see me drinking yellow coffee, dear, dear things... I'm a dunker, you know."

"Never mind that," interjetted the impatient Kraken. "Those pleasant little minnows there—" indicating the orphans, who were now contentedly belting one another with the planks their steaks had come on, "I know damn well that their shoes will fit me. Only thing is, I wouldn't want to hurt their feelings. . . so I guess I'll have to eat them first."

"Oh, I understand perfectly, perfectly, Mrs. Herbcrest," the lady said soothingly. "Just let me set this tray down somewhere, and I'll pitch right in and help you. For after all, Agatha, you *are* the president of our little welfare club."

To your true bird-watcher few events can arouse quite the same excited comment as the spectacle of a newly hatched brood of cowey-grackles floating serenely on a set of rusty old bed-springs.

HOW PEPPER CAME TO BE DISCOVERED

The door which separated the three rooms opened and a boy carrying a large bronze vessel and a scales such as cowl-weavers use entered. He looked tired and about him. The leafy curtains flapped through the boarded up windows in the direction of the orchard. Someone had made an effort to cover a series of gaping holes in the wall by plastering strips of folded newspapers over them, but now these were yellowed and revealed minute scratches across more than one bathing beauty. While through the shattered panel of the door, a heavy, shiny-badged face could be dimly seen, as well as the tip of an ink-stained ear. A fire of sticks in a copper wicket swung from the charred rafters, in this fashion providing the only illumination. In the castle up the flag-decked river, where lived a certain lonely Queen, the above description would go a-beggaring, indeed. Toward evening, having chewed, since earliest morning, an incessant amount of very salty fish pieces, she decided to go out for a drink, one of the faucets being clogged with the undependable nose of the royal plumber.

But unfortunately in her haste she did not at once remember the river nor notice that the utensil which the senile old king had

tossed down to her from one triple-chinned, frizzy-whiskered tower window was made carelessly of straw, for it was little more than a pot-of-emergency. So after having fallen in and quite spoiled her regal gown, if not her moon-enhanced appearance, dip and redip as she might, only a dank taste like from spoiled feathers rewarded her. It was then that the head of a poor crabfisher breasted the water a little to the fore of her side, and mistaking her for one of common clay, led her at golden, blushing length to the star-tiaraed bank. It was not until many, many years later that someone happened to stumble upon the old king at the foot of a deep well, grinning broadly down upon a tin drinking cup which he had been unable to uncollapse. And at least in one humble shack in a distant and pleasant spot just around a heavily-thicketted bend in the river, there is someone whose fish are seasoned with something a bit snappier than salt.

Better to be the carelessly handled bauble of a spiny young drip, than the unused rack of some pointless old umbrella.

THE EVOLUTION OF THE HIPPOPOTAMUS

Once a horse, a gawky countryboy, a striptease queen and an old featherduster decided to set up house together in a sort of windmill which had been newly remodeled to their purpose and specifications.

Everything went along very smoothly indeed until one cold, foggy morning Orker S. Wilkins, the horse, took it into his thick head to try out for the local swimming team. — "All for the glit o' a few cheap and sordid medals," as Fu-Fu Rita chose to express the general sentiment.

So nothing, of course, would do but they must all leave off where they were and go trudging up Old Sorghum Holler to the 'Grocknest Invitational', with R. C. Dasey, the countryboy, a-clutching a rusty hayfork in one hand and Granny Turkis in the other.

Oh, it was cruel! most cruel! How those rural people chortled and guffawed when poor Wilkins, that swollen with a false and silly pride as to have quite forgotten to cut a tail-hole in his suit, proceeded to plunge out into the very middle of the river—only to ignominiously drown!

Returned to the garish merry-go-round, the three survivors

sadly gawked or shapely-strippered or fluttered rather dankly, each after his or her individual fashion. Before long, however, Granny Turkis, gnawing slyly on the handle of her wire-feathered duster, remarked: "He-he-he— Heh... Oh that golldinged silly boy Wilkins! He just never did have no fair chance to outgrow that ticklish tendency of his, no-how... Go easy on the aqua with my next one, R. C. Hell, that's the least we kin do for him now..."

Even a sieve is water-tight at the bottom of a deep well.

THE HOTEL BLUES

Maimie, Jillanne, Pretty Thing, Doris Ebikuzhlavshy and the Nanary Bell have come on a routine visit. They are arguing much too noisily, and smoking long, black, lace-fringed cigarettes. One of the Sklegg boys (perhaps Tim or Little Nob) is with them, but since he is just along to look down the fronts of their blouses, he is content to say nothing. Even though, in that same lobby, stands a penniless clerk named Lemuel Clayfoot who has had the uncommon bad luck to fall in love with a rich old garment known fat and wide as Mrs. Thistledown.

To be sure, they are now in the midst of trying to figure out what to do with Lem's svelte-structured young wife, for most happily old Thissie is already safely locked up in a wall vault in his own private den. "I suppose we could tell her that we are only going off together to hunt leopards with elephants," suggested the loot-smitten clerk the next morning. (As it happened, he had just discovered a secret panel some hundred and eighty soft brown feet to the left of the vault.)

"That would hardly be fair," sighed Mrs. Thistledown, as she scraped her heavily rouged, piebald nag out from under a low-hanging branch, and rode baldly on ahead. "For the elephant is a bit bigger, don't you know."

Lem, rising abruptly to the occasion of finding still another set of her teeth on his saddle, besides the one which had lodged itself down his neck when they had stopped last near an old hollow log to change her splintered leg, declared, "I do get the impression, what with your obvious belief in full preparedness, that we should have a very peaceful time of it together." And spurring his steed stealthily back to the mansion, Clayfoot sped down to the gameroom and wrenched the panel open all in one gulp, greeting each of the ninety dancing girls warmly by name as she floated like an unusually clear September Morn forth into his arms.

Fear the united from the front, the democracy from the arsenal, and the general bringing up any rear save his own.

HOW THE SLINGSHOT CAME TO BE INVENTED

A Leopard, whose glasses had been fitted in a most helter-high-water fashion, went out one gray day a-deering, and in his short-sighted haste chanced to make prey of a Missionary's Spouse. Whereupon the latter said:

"Oh Huldred dear, I wonder if you would very much mind leaving your work long enough to come and save me. . .?"

Great sibilant leaves that were tanned a deep, brooding turtle color by long exposure to 'old-him-mucha-blig-bright-fellah-dam-dam-maybeso-allasame-me-pore-hurryhup-heathem-blast-ard' (the colorful native way of saying sun), stirred like a flutter of kneecaps on the knobby limbs of the boombah palms which could be dimly discerned through the smokehole of an empty hut near the outskirts of the village. Here, stretched to bursting upon a hammock made of discarded inner tubes, sleeps the kindly old Chief Rango Buum in an orange tuxedo with white lapels and leg stripes, which is at least more than several sizes too small for him; while a couple small brown feet away creeps ever nearer and nearer a penknife held laughingly in the little fist of one of his four hundred-odd sons, the even ones having all long since been declared illegitimate and sold off to a pet shop whose

speciality is catering to the better class of angel. Some distance removed the sky has the unmistakeable air of someone lying on a rush mat with a lovely, sixteen year old maiden, against whose shimmering, tight fitting skin great blossoms of flashing teeth-of-paradise look very shabby indeed.

After what might be considered a seemly interval the Missionary inquired, not unkindly: "Uh-err... Did I hear you say something just then, Agnes?"

"Why, yes, I hope you did, Reverend," answered his wife, her words punctuated by a series of mounting growls. "It was my thought that you might see your way to dropping your work for a moment, and so find yourself in a better position to come into the jungle a bit for the purpose of saving me; ouch—"

Then running pensive fingers through the fragrant leaves of dark blossoms, and with a somewhat impatient glance over a soft and very pretty shoulder, Huldred the Missionary said, "But really now, Agnes. I must say— it hardly impresses me as being fitting and proper that I should have made an arduous, self-annulling journey half again around this sinful earth for the rather commonplace mission of saving *you*, my dear."

But, as it happened, his solicitude, by reason of a succession of fortuitous events, went almost unnoticed. For perhaps the most circumstantial of these, in the unfettered person of good Chief Rango Buum, descended without further ado on the galvanized back of Bertie Enner Gene the ooth, whose teeth we have forgotten to say had been fitted by that same nervous optometrist. And with a violent nod at the Missionary's help-meat, whom another of his odd little sons was helping up with a homemade bugle-bagpipe combination, the kindly old Chief went hastily riding off through a huge bolo-bongo tree. On which happy note we, too, must take our leave of the great and mysterious jungle's vociferously colorful and rapidly clearing.

MOONSHINE AND HAWGJOWL

On a stool in the Lady of the Black Lilies Lunchroom, having a cuppa easy on the canned cowjuice cawffee, Buck Reluquerro glanced at the classy little blonde gentereen who was unselfconsciously rubbing an overflow of lipstick off on the front of his lemon-pink shirt.

While outside. . .

A strung-out cluster of pigeons peeling in the moldy gray sun — or are they houses? and fluttering bunches of molting grapes . . . clacking their thin beaks over scaling backfences— or are they perhaps a gossip of a slightly rarer feather, with their markings of interminable brooms and mops and buckets and tales? And across the street three men leisurely flying from a hardware, heaped-up screens on their little bawling boy-drawn cart.

Sometimes the world almost seems too big damn fine and sassy. . .

Dressed stylishly in a cut-away frock of a brilliant, faded boatred, like the underside of a rubber parrot swathed in wilting rose petals, an old lady mowing figure eights in Mayor Stallfetter's lawn. While in the arbor behind the new shoemaker's, a scene of mounting slacktivity, — much as you might expect to

265

find in a place that had just been left by eleven half-asleep giant-esses, each more eager than the last to leave nothing worldover behind. . .

So Buck Reluquerro introduced himself to his pleasant little stool-mate and said:

"Yeah, same here. Thought I hadn't seen you around town before. Well, anyway, this time I'm telling you about, my old man was out back watering up the pigs when I drove in with Erebella. She was my day-old bride, see. At eighty Pa still makes a lotta folks chuckle when they first meet him. That's because since my Maw died he's taken up the idea that he's one of them old fashioned iron bathtubs where come a Saturday night the whole family kin wash all at once. Course they's always someone round to encourage a person like that, only in his case it's the whole blame hebang of Sauley brothers. They humor him along-like — eatin' the grub right outten his old saggy mouth, sleepin' seven-teen abreast in his old sassy bunk, and twiceth the week plumb half drownin' the old boy into the bargain.

"An', like I'm tellin' you, just as I git Erebella dragged up to them, where they be round the pigs, Pa is a-sayin', 'See thet? I told you fellers my overflow valve was a-gittin' clogged.' An' one of them Sauley brothers he says, 'Shall's I let this little red-eyed hawg up thin?'

"Then I says, 'Pa', I says, 'I want fur you to meet my new one-day-old wife. Pa Reluquerro, I want's you should meet the new Mrs. Reluquerro.'

"So without turnin' round at all, Pa he says, 'Buck, you git me thet big wrench from the bucket on the mantel beside yer Uncle Pludgurkle's photey. En if she's not thear, try under them wet towels we got on top of your Maw down in the cellarway.'

"So I says, 'Noaw don't you be gittin' too onreckonable, Pa,' I says. 'I've brung Erebella all the ways from Kalamazoo just on purpose she should meet you.'

"'*Whall!*' Pa he says real loud like, an' he cradles his arms and his legs up-like to show just how pleased he is. 'Buck, yer're a right smart boy! A chip offen the old tub, even iffin I do say so!' An', I'm a sonofa old saggy gray owl with busted suspenders if Pa don't smile right up at my Erebella. An' Pa he says, 'Yessir! Yer a-lookin' at a expert, Ma'am, iffen I do say so m'self. They's oney one model better than what them Kalamazooers be— an' thet's a double bottomed Flint Imperial! Whall! m' purty little ladykins, yer a-lookin' at a good old double bottomed Flint Imperial *right this guddumed minute!*'

"So just then Wilber Sauley— he was standin' three brothers in an' chawin' baccky all up and down ole Snouty Ike's neck

267

(he's the shy one, I think I told you)— So Wilbur he says, 'Would ye like a bit of fresh-yestidey cutplug, Ma'am, Erebell-ford, please Ma'am?' But— Pa he went right on a-talkin' to my little store-boughten-like bride, an' Pa he says, 'Right after sup-per, remind me to take a look over your outlet screen. . .'

"I told you easy on that cow, Mac. So's like I was sayin', my Erebella she goes a-tearin' back to the car, darn near a-takin' half of my arm with her, an' she jumps in thet hard the motor and both front wheels come a-flyin' off, an' she kicks out the floorboards with them little purple dancin' shoes of hers— Yeah, with the mustard this time. An' fust thing we know there she is hightailin' it down that old saggy road a-blowin' one of them big purty four notes an' a blue rooster's tail horns thet I jest paid me out my last twenty-nine dollars on for all she's worth!"

Haste, if we are to believe all we hear, is the proof that always seems to go a-chasin' off to spoil somebody else's pudding for us.

THE PROFESSIONAL SON

A Candle-Sniffer was returning happily from a miss adventure when he had the fortune to encounter two well balanced cyclists propelling an old lady before them on the gleaming handlebars of their bikes. "If you don't mind me putting my cent in," he said through taut nostrils, "it strikes me you fellows could come up with something rather more interesting to do at this hour." And, with a rapid flick of his forked tongue over his waxy mustache, he smiled a gay reminiscence.

To which counsel the disheveled but happily rapt passenger made instant rejoinder, "Conceivably you are unaware that only as recently as twenty minutes ago our roles presented a somewhat identically contrary appearance. But, even if I was sure you understood that, my fine flame topped boy, what possible point could be made by reminding you— and I must insist on laying considerable stress on this— Where was I? oh yes: *ouch!* What point, indeed? Nevertheless I really feel that I should make it very clear to you that nearly all of the present merriment of these two, er, ah, gentlemen, stems from a circumstance which is no longer tenable, to say the very most."

And with that the little party disappeared around a wall.

The Candle-Sniffer waited until the last floating remnants of the warm seats had dissolved under the cold, dawn breath of a truckload of disgruntled pigs, then thoughtfully he observed, "Who'd ever have figured such a very dried-up old party would have gams long enough to pedal one of them old fashioned style high wheel jobs all by herself— let alone balance a couple fat, bad breathed grizzle bears on her forebars."

"But what I don't get," said a policeman, who had caught a hurried glimpse of the scene from his perch on a fire escape under a lighted bedroom, "is why them fellers both had big yeller hair ribbons on their tails, like."

"Hair ribbons!" exclaimed the Candle-Sniffer in the tone of one coming to his senses. "They wasn't no hair ribbons— Those was the toes out of my poor old mother's socks! I'd recognize them anywhere!" And with a fondly possessive tug at his radiant nose, he groaned fairly, "Can you beat it! After all these years — just as Paw always predicted she would— she's finally gone and got herself tired of bein' in the navy... But she would enlist! She would enlist!"

At that moment the truck squealed to a stop and a pig, considerably bolder and taller than its compatriots, began contentedly to munch on the unsuspecting policeman's leg.

It is far better to take an ice-cold shower any day than to sit out on the front lawn in a half tepid washboiler full of eels all making a great pretense of taking their own temperatures.

THE VERY BEST SALESMEN ARE NOT BORN

A short man chewing vigorously at a yard long alder branch was pulling his grandfather along on a green and yellow child's sled through the chief thoroughfare of Bearswah one fine morning recently. Bearswah, which had never been much more than a halfhearted waystation for stray brewers casing the lush markets to the north, was hardly even a place to live, or get older, sadder, come to no useable conclusion in, now. The hoary pullee felt this with especial keenity, for it was biting cold and, because of the jagged point of the stick, his sole remaining garment, a frayed scarlet woonsocket jacket, must perforce be left in relative safety on the towel shelf in Widder Nussmet's bathroom, where he and his younger kin had for so long made their surreptitious home.

It should be clearly stated here that their method of commercial congress— they were sheeps' bladder venders— had had a somewhat chance but nonetheless instantaneous evolvement; and that, further, at no more considerable cost than the loss of a succession of pairs of storebought teeth which, on that first as on all later occasions, had most effectually clamped themselves tightly round an old fashioned zinc chimney guard at the crown of the village's most prepossessing apartment house.

And so it was on this morning, as usual, that Senator Higgis V. Q. Vealfoot, his eyes bugging up like so many pale watery blue caps on a couple miniature quarts of frozen milk, gazed now warmly aloft at that jagged spur of the chimney guard, that mute and rusty testimonial to the surpassing goodness of (as the Senator always said it over rapturously to himself) That Damn Same Nice Big Fellow-Boy: for it must be made clear that to him it was the symbol of far more than any mere expediency of merchandizing: — *On the contrary, it was, in all truth, the actual and very real representation of the age old Answer itself;* something he could truly get his— well, anyway, get his "rottif ild froggie's behinder gooms intah."

So it is scarcely to be wondered at that, under impulse of the carefully wielded alder shoot, old Senator Higgis V. Q. Vealfoot, that stout hearted supersalesman and raconteur, surged impetuously upward. . . up. . . up. . . up. . . until he had gained to his accustomed place fast against the deeply pitted chimney guard— And oh then didn't he throw his voice proudly forth upon the cold morning air!

"Git yer sausage cases here-o, here-o, here-o, here-o! Yer nice fresh slaughtered sausage cases here-o, here-o. . ."

And oh is it any wonder that he paid no heed at all to doubters in the startled rooms below? Ah, yes, let them scoff all they like — "I'll hero you, you old bald bottomed reprobate!"— for the good Senator had found his chosen niche in life, and well, *ah*, how well did he know it!

A good day's hard work never hurt anybody. And especially is this true of those who make a practice of preaching this.

TAKING HOT COALS TO MISSOURI

A man in a big dusty, half-chewed hat was sitting at the bar of a honky tonk when a voice at his elbow suddenly demanded: "What are you got up in that funny rig for?"

On the point of inquiring regarding the whywithal of the stranger's unexpected interest, he turned instead to see a fellow dressed like a duck sitting right beside him. And so, he went on in a more conciliatory tone: "Whall now, partner, I be in the trade of what they call mule skinning out where I hull from."

"A mule skinner, honk?" exclaimed his new friend. "Great axe in the mornin', honk, honk! But have I got a job for you! You come right along honk with me— That damnfool wife of mine, she refuses to believe that I can turn myself into a man!"

A PASTURIZED SCENE

A little roly poly Giant Sloth chanced to be picking an bouquet of dryish blue skullcaps, when, without any warning whatever, an impetuous Cow dashed from a doorway hung with swinging bags and began at once to make wild threats against his continued safety. Much enamoured as he was by their vague, barny smell and puffy sponge-veined lips, he made in turn a most charming but nonethemore sincere gesture of offering the blossoms to her sharply divided attention. But the chuffling moocomer, who knew a sport, however natural, when she saw one, immediately thrust the poor little Giant Sloth into a nest handed her by old Bluff Durham, her ever-attentive husband, and went heelsbelling off to the market. For, you see, only the day before, while botheredly fly-ing past a shopwindow, she had noticed a pair of magnificent, shocking-pink panties, which she had every reason to believe would make her the season's most spectacular social bust.

VISIT TO A SUBURB IN HEAVEN

Tuthneda's eyes are closed, windows in a field of soft, tremblingly purple grass. . .

On one of the roofs a laugh clad saloon, its glasses fogged in a swirl of skirts. "This one's on me!" it calls; only to answer, "Watch it, Sugar— his wife's a pretty rough old dish of tea. . ." While still above that a man in a wingchair ventures a few twirling comments and, the clouds stuffed in about him more carefully, plucks up the baker's little red dog and flys off in a flurry of mounting nostalgia. Then first one building then another steps out of the graying streetscape, only to discover a tiny little princess lost asleep in its cornerstone. At which Buldy Thom, the captain of police, growls, "Ugh! just like me missus, only smaller— and a sight prettier to look at." (Just so each does one day recognize his own. For what is for one lad a toad—) Now another figure in the window above the Lobsters Club, who had been aimlessly cradling its chin in a pair of huge catsup colored pliers while watching the chorus undress in the ballrooms on its either side, breaks off as Tuthneda appears once more. For she is wonderfully enchanting! And, in fact, if the word was simply made for anybody, it was for no other but her.

A blue blue is the rain over the village. Off to the grocer's, soft basket across her flowered arm, Tuthneda trancingly goes. But not to buy any sugar sweet water biscuits or coolen of gold ale... ah no! she is only pretending to be marketing at all in order to disabuse a stern mother. And so she sings, the steeples chiming enviously in, while down the rot of shadowing wings silence leans to listen in on the unequal concert. Yet here at such a walking's end, this hut, this humble, unadorned setting— with here an empty chair, a bench unoccupied and festooned with cruel wreaths of fish lines and crab traps, and over there a table covered by an oilcloth checkered with squares of dun and darbled green. And a bed. The bed of a poor fisherman...

O as in the snowless purity of an April winter— there lies Tuthneda, in new radiance, so very prettily asleep. Ah, later... long later and then later, it will be time enough, surely more than time enough to go back through the starry mist to receive the reprimands of her unsympatico mother, who was badly shaken up in the fall of 1871*).

*) One of the least-publicized catastrophes of all history.

278

THE COCK OF ALL THE WORLD

Two olive-colored barnacle gooses waddled along the pier, complaining at being disturbed at their supper of ball-bearings and cotterkeys which they had salvaged from an accumulation of careless rollerskaters on the harbor's narrow floor. Known locally as weisswangengan, their relationship until recently had been that of mother and son. Now it would be difficult, treating of the lady first, to say which she was bigger with, guilt or egg; as for the other, foolishness seemed his most natural cover.

In her slip nearby, the *Mary Widders* was rubbing her boot-scuffed breast restlessly against *Old Jolly John*, only that morning in from Singapore, his hauser-holes still a-drip with the brackish scent of musk and untidy sandlewimps. Somewhere a man in a gay monk's cloth kimono was feeding a roll of unpunched paper into a player piano, while in the next room a well-known musical comedy composer busily cribbed down every other note; now and then, as though prodded on by an explosive clock filled with oozing milkweed, a police launch cut in and out of the jetty, leaving bits of canoes and their carefree cargoes to collect in the reddening pockets of moonlight.

And yet, *no more than a few inches in the other direction. . .* it was raining!

And there, people with silver bucketed heads were being tossed back and forth by two enormous children behind whom, his palely spotted tail covering the sky, a ghost-white rooster stood, negligently pecking at an unseen string of the kind packages of dust are said to come fastened with.

THE NUMBER THAT COMES AFTER FEVE

Just about everybody went on the picnic. (And while some were off in the fields falling prone upon gay prone*, others contented themselves with the felling of one swoop**). It might be said that what had been so often told before over the cupboard pillows, was finding new excitements in the retelling. Some $ 300, 007, 000 and 52 c worth of scenery went almost unnoticed in that sizzling Friday afternoon friskforall.

And presently, when the village was having its pre-dark highbell, and larks were beginning to light each pretty house, in that gloaming where every song was a better kind of lamp for what no bed however trundled could do alone, couple after couple— hmmm... The woods were beginning to fill with merry shadows— All there along the flower skirted river, while safely in their stalls vast sullen cows stirring mournfully. Voices were beginning slowly to make themselves heard, as someone... approached... down... the purple tumbling of the hill. "You

*) A species of little rose-chested quail, which are often mistaken in maturity for grouse.

**) An oat seldom given to domesticity— although it is occasionally to be found growing under portable Indian blankets and on the saddles of horses born, for the most part, in the last century.

name it, Susan, I'll buy a star down for you any old day." And "Come on, you big kneewet! You're just tetched in the heel, scared of every little thing— just like that bussy-jimpin' ma of yours." and "And there was Uncle Pilgus a-comin' down the lane all cake-eared from his pore ole daddy's wedding." and "So's I just staked it on the ram and come on over to look up my little whomwithal." and, far-off, the taunting of little Bilford Blister: "Mary Ellen's got a stuck on Taffi Johnson. . . Mary Ellen's got. . ."

Softly, softly, *fugit hora* with their pleasant *entremets*.

And so we to our story. . .

ALSO AVAILABLE FROM NEW DIRECTIONS

Kenneth Patchen's last words to New Directions' founder James Laughlin were, "When you find out which came first, the chicken or the egg, you write and tell me." Patchen answered the riddle by painting "picture-poems." *The Walking-Away World* contains three of his picture-poem collections: *Wonderings, Hallelujah Anyway*, and *But Even So*. Inspired by the "illuminated printing" of William Blake, Patchen worked with a spirited fervency in watercolor, casein, inks, and other media to create absurd, compelling works. His entire process was a simultaneous fusion of painting and poetry: neither the poem nor the painting preceded the other. Each picture-poem is inhabited by strange beings uttering everything from poignant poetic adages to cheeky satire. One confides, "I have a funny feeling / that some very peculiar looking creatures out there are watching us." The graphic artist and cartoonist Jim Woodring helps to capture the suspicious joys of *The Walking-Away World* with an effervescent introduction.

A New Directions Paperbook Original
NDP1114
$18.95 US/ $22.00 CAN
ISBN: 978-0-8112-1757-6

What the story tells itself
when there's nobody around
to hear it

Kenneth Patchen

What can you do up here
that you can't go on doing
just as vilely on earth?
Patchen